W9-DED-011

Getting Your
¥EN'$
Worth

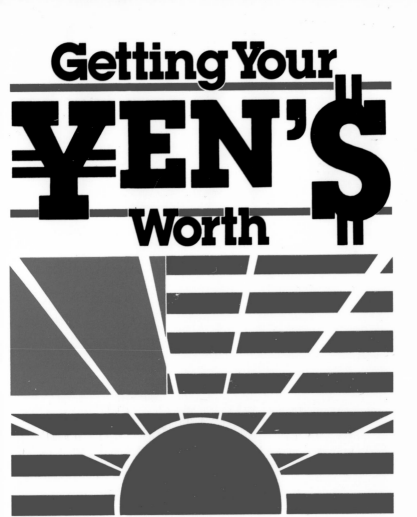

How to Negotiate
with Japan, Inc.

Robert T. Moran

WARNING: This is *not* just another book about "inscrutable" Japanese management. It *is* a success formula for going head to head with America's most competitive trading partner.

33

9.95
LOI

Getting Your
¥EN'$
Worth

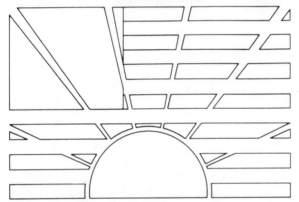

How to Negotiate
with Japan, Inc.

Robert T. Moran

Gulf Publishing Company
Book Division
Houston, London, Paris, Tokyo

Dedication

For my father and mother, who provided
many opportunities for me to learn

Getting Your Yen's Worth
How to Negotiate with Japan, Inc.

First Printing, January 1985
Second Printing, September 1987

Library of Congress
Cataloging in Publication Data

Moran, Robert T., 1938–
  Getting Your Yen's Worth.

  Includes index.
  1. United States—Foreign economic relations—United States. 2. Japan—Foreign
economic relations—United States. 3. Negotiation in business. I. Title.
II. Title: Getting Your Yen's Worth.
HF1456.5.J3M67 1984   658.4   84-10882
ISBN 0-87201-410-X

Acknowledgments

Graduate students who participated in an advanced seminar at the American Graduate School of International Management in Glendale, Arizona completed much of the research for this book. Most had never been to Japan but all, painstakingly, checked the information they gathered with Japanese businessmen for accuracy. My initial intention was to identify, by chapter, each person who researched materials for that section. However, this became impossible because of the reorganization of the researched materials. Each person listed participated in this project, and I thank them sincerely:

Bruce A. Moore
Elizabeth R. Brill
Christopher K. Estes
Lise Vidnes
Christian Ramm
Sue E. Robisch
Dorothy J. Russell
Thomas N. Harrison
Gail Warner Houck
Peter T. Higuchi
Marcella Simon Peralta
Bradley L. Swain
Tom Steven Schutter

Jean-Antoine Sanchez
Jeremy J. Umland
Shukuko Onishi
Mary E. Remmel
Bruce M. McGlasson
Karen A. Gengle
Linda Van Sickle
Pamela R. DiMeo
Basil S. Holobetz
Carol Lynn Schma
Steve Spitts
Denis Serres

I also wish to thank William Voris, president of the American Graduate School of International Management, for providing financial assistance for research and typing of the final manuscript.

Persons who read the manuscript and recommended changes based on their experiences are George Renwick (a long-time friend, who thoroughly read the entire manuscript and made challenging suggestions), Tetsuo Tobata, Yoshiatsu Takyu (a former student, and now a *kacho*, who was my teacher in many ways), Robert Shatz, Martin Sours, Katsusuke Tanaka, Alex Ying, and Shirley J. Casey.

Harry C. Jamison, president, ARCO Exploration Company, is a negotiator who insists that all sides "win" and long-term benefits are established and nurtured. I thank him for writing the foreword.

Thanks also go to Karen Johnson of Animagination Inc. for contributing the cartoons, and to my editor, Tim Calk of Gulf Publishing Company, for his many comments and clarifying questions.

Contents

A Case of Failure. A Day in the Life of a Japanese Negotiator. The Education of Japanese Businessmen. Japanese Company Selection Process. Promotion. Decision Making. Japanese Business Negotiating Courtesies. Styles of Communication. Japanese Negotiating Principles. The Role of Government. Role of Attorneys. Summary.

An Overview. The Basis of the American Value System. Applying the American Value System to Negotiations. Negotiation: American Style. Components of the Final Agreement. Number of Negotiators. Protocol—Does It Exist? Concluding Comments and Some Advice.

Analysis and Implications for American Negotiators. Japan's Past. Aspects of Japanese Management Behavior. Japanese Workers. Hierarchical Relations.

Foreword

In this book Professor Moran comes to grips with a fundamental challenge, and a paradox, which affects American business almost universally. The challenge faces every businessperson who attempts to work with people from different cultural backgrounds. The paradox occurs when the same behaviors that were successful in negotiating with other Americans lead to failure when dealing cross-culturally.

How to Negotiate with Japan, Inc. is not merely a "how to" catalogue of "do's and don't's." While Bob Moran does prescribe a strong dose of what to do and what to avoid, he also requires the reader to develop a solid foundation of knowledge, ethical behavior, ethnic understanding, and mutual respect.

His descriptions of behavioral characteristics of both Japanese and Americans in business negotiations are drawn from a long and successful first-hand involvement in such situations. Since he also has served as a consultant to domestic and foreign companies world-wide for many years, he brings a broad perspective to bear on this more specific subject.

My personal experience with Bob dates back several years when my company initiated negotiations with Japanese firms regarding petroleum exploration in the U.S. Bob gave us a crash course in general cross-cultural awareness, as well as specific approaches to follow in dealing with Japanese companies and individuals. We also learned, as you will, some of the "tried and true" tactics and methods to avoid. Although we did not reach contractual agreement at that time, we did establish long-term relationships that endure today and leave the door open for future ventures.

As a result of that experience, my company has had Bob Moran work with us on a series of cross-cultural programs involving American Indian Tribes with whom we had established, or desired to establish, business ventures. These programs include face-to-face meetings between tribal representatives and ARCO Exploration Company employees. We learn about each other's cultural background, business methods, and, most importantly, seek to establish personal rapport, which can lead to the understanding and mutual respect that underlie a good business relationship.

Bob consistently encourages treating others with sincerity and respect based upon knowledge and understanding. He advocates the pursuit of "win-win" solutions so as to create synergy. The result then is mutual satisfaction and benefit. Bob believes in these principles. I am personally convinced of their value. They work!

H. C. Jamison
President, ARCO Exploration Company

Preface

In early 1964, I arrived in Japan full of enthusiasm, energy, idealism, and a sincere desire to succeed. After living in Japan for about a year, my idealism diminished somewhat after meeting many expatriates (mostly Americans, Canadians, and Europeans) who did not speak Japanese well, did not understand the Japanese people with whom they worked and, by their own admission, did not particularly like being in Japan. "The Japanese are mysterious, complex, and too difficult to even try to understand" was the feeling of some.

Then one day, quite by accident, I met a foreigner who was fluent in Japanese. He could also read and write the language with ease, and he liked living in Japan. He told me "The Japanese are no more inscrutable than Americans. They are just different. Anyone can learn to succeed in Japan if they make the necessary effort."

By this time, I was assisting the Japanese Skating Union in helping to prepare young Japanese hockey players for the 1972 Olympic Winter Games to be held in Sapporo. At a team meeting I announced that I was changing a player in one of the forward lines. That evening during a lengthy discussion with two officials, I was told that my decision would not work in Japan because "all three players on the line graduated from the same university." I asked myself "What does graduating from the same university have to do with playing hockey?" I learned in Japan graduating from the same university does have something to do with one's ability to score goals. Different yes, inscrutable, no.

My apprenticeship continued for the next four years until I returned to the United States to begin graduate school. Since then I have returned to Japan many times and have worked with numerous Japanese businessmen. Now my conviction is even stronger . . . Japan, Inc. and Japanese businessmen are not inscrutable. In certain ways we share similar approaches. In many important ways we are different.

In discussing this project with William Lowe, editor-in-chief of Gulf Publishing Company's Book Division, he suggested "An average reader should be able to read the entire book on a flight between Los Angeles and Tokyo, with 3 hours left for snoozing." Such is the goal. Another important goal is for the material to be immediately helpful for the reader. This means reading the book and reflecting on the major points should make a positive difference in one's ability to negotiate with the Japanese.

The information was gathered primarily from three sources: first, published materials about doing business with the Japanese; second, from interviews with Americans who have worked extensively with Japanese businessmen; third, from Japanese businessmen.

Most of the many excellent books on Japan contain little information of *practical* use to the negotiator. This book is designed to fill the gap. To be included, the information had to be accurate, relevant to the negotiator, and understandable.

It is my conviction that a foreigner's knowledge of how the Japanese negotiate will enhance his ability to develop and maintain cooperative and mutually beneficial long-term commercial relationships.

Japan is like most highly industrialized countries, but deceptively so, because it has successfully blended the old—traditional cultural concepts—with the new—modern technology. Chapter 1 describes the background and values of Japanese negotiators to help you better understand the impact of this mixture. Chapter 2 does the same for U.S. negotiators to provide a basis for comparison. Chapter 3 provides insight into how Japanese perceive American negotiators—seeing ourselves as they see us is a preliminary but critical aspect of developing effective negotiating skills. Ground rules and "secrets" of successful negotiations are presented in Chapters 4, 5, and 6 so that proper preparations can be made. Chapter 7 covers the negotiating session itself—what you are likely to encounter when you are sitting at the negotiating table, face to face with your Japanese counterparts. Entertainment, an important activity in the Japanese business world, is addressed in Chapter 8. Chapter 9 examines how the Japanese approach contract negotiations and focuses on specific areas of potential dispute. Chapter 10 provides some brief exercises/checklists for helping you determine your preparedness in negotiating with the Japanese: and Chapter 11 describes the challenge of dealing with "Japan, Inc." and suggests ways to meet that challenge. The appendices contain a negotiating style questionnaire for self-assessment and a list of information sources and recommended reading.

Robert T. Moran

Introduction

JAPAN

Population:	119,000,000*
Capital:	Tokyo, population 12,000,000
G.N.P.:	$1.1 trillion (U.S.)
Unemployment:	2.5 percent
Inflation:	2.2 percent

1983 — The second most powerful economy in the free world.
1990 — May achieve a per capita G.N.P. greater than the United States.

"Japanese negotiators are more skilled than any group of businessmen I have worked with from any country."

Comment by a U.S. business negotiator

"MacArthur: Japan Doomed As World Power

. . . Japan will never again become a world power, Gen. Douglas MacArthur said today in an interview with United Press.

'Japan industrially, commercially, militarily and every other way is in a state of complete collapse.' "

San Mateo Times
San Mateo, California
September 21, 1945

This book is about Japan—the *second most powerful economy in the free world*—and how its negotiators negotiate.

It is hard to find a more unlikely partnership than the Japan-U.S. relationship that has developed since the end of WWII. Japan is a homogeneous society about the size of California. The United States is a "melting pot" of persons from many countries.

I take the position that Japanese negotiators are neither infinitely complex nor are they simple economic entities and pawns of Japan, Inc. They are businessmen as are their foreign counterparts. (I use the masculine pronoun because unlike the business world in the United States, almost all Japanese negotiators are men. The same is generally true of Americans who negotiate with the Japanese, although an increasing number are women.) Both are rooted in their cultures. However, Japanese negotiators have a different past and a different present. In order for Western businessmen to negotiate successfully with their Japanese counterparts, they must understand how the past influences the present.

How Japan became an economic world power accounting for 10% of the world's industrial output will not be explained; much has already been written on that. This book focuses on negotiating. It is intended to present information that American negotiators can apply when negotiating with the Japanese. The contrasting values, styles, behaviors, philosophies, and strategies of U.S. negotiators are presented in Chapter 2.

There seems to be an increasing inability for Americans to sell products in the Japanese marketplace. This persists despite growing American international trade and many technologically superior products. Explanations for this failure vary, but most are presented at the macroeconomics level; i.e., government interferences, tariffs, or quotas. Some of these explanations contain an element of truth, but one must also ask how much of the problem is a result of the American negotiator's skill at negotiating. Anthropologist Edward T. Hall states in *The Dance of Life:* "When the American executive travels abroad to do business, he is frequently shocked to discover to what extent the many variables of foreign behavior and customs complicate his efforts." Indeed, the difficulty of cross-cultural transactions is perhaps manifested most commonly at the negotiation table.

This problem was expressed by *Time* in its special issue on "Japan—A Nation in Search of Itself" when they wrote:

> "The knot tightens in the Western businessman's stomach as he peers glumly at the Japanese negotiating team across the table."
>
> *Time* August 1, 1983

Why is it difficult negotiating with Japanese businessmen? Japanese negotiators are polite, vague, exceedingly well prepared and determined to make the best possible deal.

A Japanese businessman who was assisting Westerners to understand Japan compared his country and people to a swan. He said, "Japanese are like swans in a pond. On the surface everything is serene and well controlled. But the feet are moving very rapidly even though they cannot be seen. You Westerners must see our feet if you wish to understand us."

Many books have been written about Japan and some of the most recent are listed in the suggested readings. The information in Chapters 1–10 is a bare-bones presentation—information without which one is not even prepared in a preliminary sense to work with Japanese negotiators. The material also suggests why "the knot tightens" as Western negotiators meet with their Japanese counterparts. Japan has a different history and a different present.

Glossary of Japanese Words

Amae—A desire for security. It involves a sublimation of one's self-interests for the security and protection of the group. The result has been a people deeply group conscious, constantly striving for the ideals of harmony and unanimity.

Amakudari—Appointment of a former government employee to a private company.

Bucho—Division chief.

O-chugen—The midsummer time of year when gift-giving is popular.

Kokkai—Japanese version of our Congress. Composed of two levels, the upper is the House of Councilors, the lower is the House of Representatives.

Gakubatsu—University connections, which are very important in Japan's class-oriented society. Indicative of the elitist nature of Japanese management.

Honne—"True mind" or "saying it like it is." All too often, Japanese are reluctant to offer their true feelings, thinking to do so will offend the listener.

Ie—The family model imposed on the Japanese male and affects extrafamilial relationships. It features male domination, female submission, and respect for elders.

Jinmyaku—The cult of personal connections vital to the success of the *zaikai*. Industrial organizations often are the stage for the strongest ties. Also may include political, social, and educational organizational ties.

Kacho—Department chief, or manager.

Karaoke—Literally means "empty orchestra." These are popular Japanese songs recorded with no vocals. Late in the evening, men will sing in bars as more spirits are consumed.

Keibatsu—Extended familial connections.

Keidanren—The Federation of Economic Organizations. In 1981, it included 110 industrial organizations. Strongest in the fields of iron and steel, vehicles, shipbuilding, petrochemicals, electronics, and electrical power generation.

Keizai Doyukai—Committee for Economic Development. Conducts national level policy discussions and seminars for many managers throughout Japan.

Kinmyaku—Money connections. Based upon *zaikai* contributions to political organizations and politicians.

Madogiwa-zoku—Literally, "people sitting next to the window." Rather than being fired, many senior workers are "kicked upstairs" to positions of no responsibility.

Nemawashi—Process of detailed informal and formal discussions before a decision is made.

Nikkeiren—Japan Federation of Employers' Associations. Principal labor union negotiators for over 50 industrial organizations, including over 29,000 individual companies and 10 million workers.

Nissho—The Japanese Chamber of Commerce and Industry. The oldest, but least influential, of the *zaikai* organizations. *Nissho* represents the interests of small to medium-sized firms.

O-miyage—Literally means "gift." But has come to mean souvenirs. Each region of Japan is known for its *o-miyage*.

Oyako—Father-son model. The method by which a new employee is integrated into the department work group or the corporate family by an older, more experienced employee.

Ringi sho—The consensus style of decision making used by most Japanese firms. Involves total involvement in decision making from bottom to top. The result is a thorough but also lengthy process.

Senpai-Kohai Relationship—A corollary of *oyako*. This is on the blue-collar level and broadly applies to white collar employees as well.

Tatemae—The peculiar characteristic of Japanese to withhold true feelings in favor of stating what they think the listener "wants to hear."

Zaibatsu—Major business cartels, often with interwoven family ties. The zaibatsu were broken up by U.S. occupation authorities after World War II.

Zaikai—The upper strata of Japanese corporate structure. Sometimes called "Japan, Inc." Literally means "the financial world."

1

Background and Values of Japanese Negotiators

A Case of Failure*

*T*erry Warner is a successful American businessman who is much admired by his colleagues for his ability to negotiate difficult deals. His frank, open, and un-compromising manner has earned him a great deal of respect at the bargaining table. Last year, he was sent by his corporation to Japan to negotiate an important contract. However, he had no experience in Asia and only very little knowledge of the business culture of Japan, although he has read of their high productivity. He was confident that he would be successful, as both sides had already agreed on many important points.

The trip was a disaster. Not only did the contract not get signed, but Terry was unable to explain why he failed. He returned to the United States frustrated, angry, and with the feeling that the Japanese business system is the most frustrating one he had ever encountered.

Introduction

The information in this chapter will help you avoid being another Terry Warner; it is intended to reduce your failures and increase your successes.

---

* Based on the actual experiences of a U.S. company in Japan.

In order to facilitate the success of business negotiations with the Japanese, it is vital that American negotiators be aware of and prepared to deal with Japanese negotiators' patterns of behavior.

One important feature of Japanese behavior is the way in which emotions are handled. Howard Van Zandt in his article "How to Negotiate in Japan" gives this example of the different role of emotions in a business relationship:

> "Recently a friend came to my office bringing a small potted Chinese bamboo. He explained that in his garden was a large bamboo which had had a baby. He carefully nourished the little one until it was big enough to put in a pot and bring to me. He advised me on its care."

Japanese negotiators are also quite skillful in concealing negative emotions. Professor Chie Nakane of Tokyo University, after studying behavior patterns of the Europeans, Indians and Americans, notes that the emotional expression of the Japanese is comparable to that of the Italians. One difference, she remarks, is that while the Italian's display of emotions may have nothing whatever to do with anyone in particular, the Japanese expression of emotion is decidedly directed towards or against a specific cause or individual. Interestingly, despite the Japanese emotional sensitivity, negative feelings of Japanese are often difficult for Americans to detect.

Japanese negotiators are also noted for their dislike of power displays. In negotiations, the Japanese are very capable of and prefer conciliation, as opposed to alienation. Differences are settled in a manner so that no one "loses face."

The Japanese prefer to work in groups rather than alone, which, some say, has lead to their economic success. Whereas the American is apt to attribute business success to individual knowledge and effort, the Japanese are more apt to attribute negotiation success to working together. An American may say "*I* did it," whereas a Japanese would say "*We* did it."

The system of decision making in Japan is one based on concensus. A formalized proposal is passed both upward and horizontally in the hierarchy. Ultimately, the proposal reaches the president, where it receives an official stamp. The key to this system, however, is that as authority is distributed among the lower tiers of the hierarchy, everyone feels that he is contributing to the decisions. This will be described in more detail in this chapter.

The trait of not saying "no" is one that confuses most Westerners. According to Professor Nakane:

> "Expression of 'no' is virtually never used outside of completely reciprocal relationships, and from superior to inferior. You rarely receive a 'no' from a Japanese, even when he means 'no' he would use 'yes' in the verbal form."

Learning verbal cues for "no" in the Japanese language takes the foreigner a long time. When a Japanese is feeling pressured to give an answer, he may draw breath through his teeth and say "sah" (no meaning), or a slightly less ambiguous response, "it is very difficult." In both cases, the negotiator probably means "no." An example illustrates how the Japanese use "yes" when the answer is "no"—even, if only to be polite.

> "I recall well a case where a visitor obtained a commitment from a Japanese concern to take some action. But, after the visitor had boarded his plane for Honolulu, the president of the Japanese company told me: 'I know, of course, that we cannot carry out our promise, but I didn't want to hurt his feelings and spoil his trip. Now you must cable him and explain it can't be done!' "

> (Van Zandt: 1970: p. 51)

The Japanese tradition of telling people what they think will please them rather than being negative is a potentially difficult situation unless the American negotiator learns to handle it with tact. The most effective way to deal with it, says Van Zandt, is to conceal the answers one wishes to hear.

Negative questions also cause misunderstandings for negotiators. For example:

American: "Do you want to play golf this weekend?"
Japanese: "Yes, I want to play golf this weekend."
Japanese: "Yes, I don't want to play golf this weekend."

For a Japanese, "yes" does not always mean "yes," and "no" does not always mean "no." "Yes" may simply mean I understand the question.

Another example—An American says, "Osaka is *not* the capital of Japan." A Japanese nods his head, which means that he understood or "that's right." He's thinking, "Yes, I understand that Osaka is *not* the capital of Japan," or "I agree that Osaka is *not* the capital of Japan." In Western countries, a Japanese should shake his head and say "No, it is not."

Close friends are very important in order for Japanese to feel secure. There are, however, varying degrees of friendship. Professor Nakane states:

> "The relative strength of the human bond tends to increase in proportion to the length and intensity of actual contact. The reason the newcomer in any Japanese group is placed at the very bottom of the hierarchy is that he has the shortest period of contact. This is a primary condition of the seniority system, which dominates Japan. Therefore, the placement of an individual in a social group is governed by the length of the individual's contact with the group. In other words, the actual contact itself becomes the individual's private social capital . . ."

Another trait of the Japanese usually not understood by Westerners is their reluctance to argue. A Japanese will not discuss a point when he feels that he is correct. While this trait could be mistaken for close-mindedness, or stubbornness of character, it should be accepted as a quality that must be "negotiated around."

A Day in the Life of a Japanese Negotiator*

The ability to walk in the shoes of another is called empathy. Before reading about the education, training, and negotiating strategies used by Japanese negotiators, read the following passages from the diary of a Japanese to give you a "feel" for your negotiating counterparts.

March
My alarm clock rang at seven as usual. I am sleepy. Every night, I came home too late, especially last night at two in the morning. I drank a lot with my customer.

---

* Taken from the diary of a Japanese negotiator and used with permission. The information in brackets [ ] is added to provide explanatory background.

Although drinking with the customer is a part of my job, I have to be on time for work the next morning.

It is Friday today. Nothing special for the Japanese businessman. [On Saturdays, 60% of Japanese companies still open their business as well as some government sectors.] My company has a five-day week program, but last year I only took six days of Saturdays for my holidays.

I did not have enough time to eat breakfast this morning. I stayed in bed too long. More and more businessmen eat breakfast at a station-stall rather than at home. We just eat one bean-jam bun and drink a bottle of milk. In winter, we can see a long line in front of the *soba-ya* at the station.

April

Sunday is my day for rest. I used to be in bed until eleven or noon. Japanese breakfast style has been changing. TV commercials say, "Put tomato juice on the breakfast table," and "before breakfast, let's drink vegetable juice."

After napping, I took a walk. On the way, I stopped by Pachinko Parlor. [Pachinko is a pin-ball game and is a very popular recreation among Japanese businessmen.] One time I played for eight hours and during this period, I did not eat anything. We businessmen concentrate on shooting the balls in order to forget our anxieties at work. [Pachinko balls can be exchanged for things such as cigarettes, chocolates, canned food, detergents, etc. Now, there are some special Pachinkos parlors that are bigger than supermarkets and have vegetables, fruits, toiletries, magazines, books, and even underwear.]

After taking a walk, I went to a golf driving range, but I had to wait for two hours. So, I gave up practicing today. We need reservations a week in advance to secure a place on the driving range.

May

This afternoon, I made a business call to the president of a major client with my two bosses. At that time, I remembered the business etiquette that I learned in the training period.

When we are served tea, the order of drinking is the president first, the director, *bucho, kacho,* and then myself. When we leave the room, we have to put the lid on the teacup.

Around ten o'clock in the evening, I was at the Narita International Airport. The president's daughter was going abroad. I was standing at the customs entrance with a flower basket because my client's favorite subject of conversation was his daughter's achievements.

In my business diary, the birthdays of my clients, their wives, and even of their children are listed. [From that information, the Japanese businessman makes a gift plan. For example, graduation or entrance to a new school are good reasons for sending a small gift.]

June

I am very surprised to see many older employees who are working, but are losing their worth living. The number of *madogiwa-zoku* [literal translation is "people sitting next to the window"] has been increasing. [These people are assigned to very boring and unconstructive jobs and forced to work all day facing the window without any hope of promotion.]

July

This morning, the personnel changes in our company were announced. We are often moved around not only all over Japan but abroad. My manager was promoted to our Sapporo office. Although he has to move alone because of his children's education and other problems such as housing and taking care of parents, he cannot refuse this assignment. If he refuses it, his life with the company will not be happy. [Even when Japanese employees are sent abroad for a long period, it is not unusual for his wife and family to remain in Japan for the sake of the children's education. If the children go to school abroad, their education would be handicapped by their deficiency in their new language, and it would be extremely difficult for them to catch up with their classmates upon returning to Japan. This has become an increasingly difficult problem for Japanese multinationals.]

August

I plan to take a summer vacation. Last summer, I took four days. Nearly 80% of *kacho* said they cannot forget work during vacation, and they become worried about work if their vacation exceeds three days.

September

Today, I went to play golf with my customers at Utsuno-miya Country Club. I had to get up at 3:30 a.m., although last night I went to bed at 1:00 a.m. First of all, I picked my boss up, then went to my client's house. On the way to the golf course, we are talking about many things, even business matters.

We bet chocolates on the game. One chocolate is worth Y500 [$2.50]. I would not be allowed to win the game, or play it stupidly, because they are clients. Sometimes, we play 19 holes. [The 19th hole is played on a green table called a *mahjongg*.] If I won the golf game, I would be expected to lose the mahjongg. If I lost the golf game, I should lose the mahjongg too.

October

I had to install our products for a customer who owns fashion boutiques in Tokyo. This owner is a so-called career woman.

November

It was fun to drink with my colleagues in the small shops [*aka-cho-chin* or *yakitori-ya*]. Our topics on drinking are always about our bosses. Last night, we were talking about just one of our bosses.

> My friend: "That manager makes me mad."
>   Me: "He is not good at his job, he is always kissing his boss's ass."

My friend: "He likes to chase skirts, too. He has no business holding that job."

Me: "I cannot stand to work for someone like that."

My friend: "That's right, that's right, let's get drunk."

Suddenly our boss appeared.

Boss: "Good evening. May I join you?"

My friend: "Oh, Kacho-san, what a pleasure to see you, please join us, we are just saying how happy we are to have you as our boss."

Me: "You are always so good to us."

Boss: "Do you think so? As a matter of fact, the present director is incompetent, all he is good for is bullshitting."

My friend: "That's right, he is impotent and bold."

[This kind of conversation would continue until midnight.]

How is this businessman educated, selected, and trained? The answers follow.

The Education of Japanese Businessmen

A fundamental objective of Japanese education is to prepare the student to become an exemplary citizen and a model worker in the company. This education begins in the home, where the child learns the essence of the Japanese culture. At an early age, he learns the importance of courteousness, consideration, and self-discipline. These attributes carry over into all aspects of life from family life to school to the working world.

The top companies in Japan select their employees from the best universities and competition for admittance to these schools is fierce. Students are admitted on the basis of their scores on an entrance examination. These examinations evaluate the student's ability to study and use intelligence rather than simply measure their level of intelligence. Much of the educational system at the primary, middle, and high school level is geared to preparing students for the college entrance examinations.

Preparation for the exams begins with enrolling the child in the best possible elementary school. Students attend supplementary schools (on Saturdays or after school) while they are in elementary or secondary school to better prepare themselves for the entrance examinations to the best and most prestigious high schools.

Much of a Japanese student's life revolves around the preparation for the examinations. Ezra Vogel in *Japan as Number 1* states:

> These examinations have the advantage of setting a certain standard, the student internalizes attitudes about hard work, and his strong relation to his peer group, to his family, to his teachers and they to him. As a result, the motivation to study is greatly reinforced.

Due to its well-developed educational system, Japan has a competent and well-educated work force. Even after completing college the desire to continue to learn is reflected in the Japanese affinity for reading and participation in correspondence courses.

Although companies reward creativity and ingenuity, the emphasis of the Japanese educational system is on learning what has been established rather than on innovation.

The following comparison in education between Japan and the United States is useful:

Japan	United States
☐ 240 days of school per year	☐ 180 days of school per year
☐ Illiteracy—less than 1%	☐ Illiteracy—about 8%
☐ 99% of entering students complete high school	☐ 80% of entering students complete high school
☐ Students follow guidelines and do not develop originality	☐ Creative thinking is encouraged
☐ Memorization	☐ Logical thinking
☐ No verbal presentations	☐ Presentation skills emphasized

Japanese Company Selection Process

Most large companies in Japan offer lifetime employment to about 30% of their employees. Barring serious long-term economic depression, these employees expect never to be laid off. If a company dissolves or merges with another company, the employees expect that new jobs will be arranged for them.

Japanese management emphasizes the long-term results of its policies. By keeping employees for life and involving them in the plans and decisions of the company, management feels employees will develop a sense of loyalty for the company and take pride in their work.

Japanese companies also provide a sense of belonging to their employees. Life revolves around the company. Every workday begins with a brief exercise period with the purpose of building confidence and pride. Company gymnasiums, swimming pools, and sports facilities are provided by many companies for use during the exercise period or after-work hours; and the immediate effect of exercising is that the employee has more energy and stamina to carry out a full day's work.

Japanese companies are committed to their employees and provide them with a sense of belonging and personal support. Japanese companies have also achieved a level of success in motivating their employees to continuously do their best. As a result, employees are motivated to produce since they believe that their future success lies in the success of their company.

Promotion

Promotion and salary increases are mainly determined by the number of years in the company. However, education, productiveness, and cooperation are also considered. Top management positions are awarded to those with the greatest ability, the broadest experience, and the longest years of service. Older workers typically hold top management positions.

The hiring procedure for new employees is as follows: The calendar year in government, business, and education is from April 1 to March 31 (of the following year). Hiring is done once a year with the procedure starting about October 1st. First, there is a written examination, which is followed by personal interviews and a health examination. About April 1, most companies have a "welcome party" for new employees and an "orientation" that lasts one or two weeks. Speakers are various department managers and the subjects covered are company policy, company profile, personnel practices, and company rules and regulations.

New employees often begin as "shop floor workers" even if they are being groomed to be managers. To gain an understanding of the Japanese management structure, employees work at all levels of management. With sufficient seniority the employee will be able to direct a department of the company. By having worked at all levels of management, the employee will have gained valuable insight and contacts and will be prepared to advance to a leadership position. Most senior officers in Japanese banks started as tellers.

The training will last for several years. During the training period the company becomes the worker's life. Often, new employees live in company dormitories. Japanese workers internalize the company ideology—the company is their home away from home so they accept the present psychic investment in anticipation of future capital appreciation. From the Japanese point of view, there are two reasons for the strong, loyal worker attitude of the Japanese worker: (1) to show appreciation for their lifetime employment status; and (2) they want to move up in the company. Japanese are trained to work in a group or as a team. As a result, the Japanese are much more dedicated and loyal to other members of a Japanese team, no matter what happens. This loyalty provides the foundation for future relationships. Japanese employees are trained to depend on each other and especially upon their seniors since they can act as mentors.

Group effort takes on great importance. In Japan one rarely accomplishes anything by oneself. It may be that one person initiates the action or does the majority of work, but it is necessary to involve others so that the overall feeling of group effort and achievement is shared. Learning who to involve and how to include them is a long and tedious process.

The new employee experiences long periods of specific training with proper humble status. Working in groups, an ability developed at an early age, is an activity that an employee will frequently participate in throughout this training period and his career. Learning from fellow workers as well as visitors is a skill developed extensively throughout a Japanese employee's career.

A new employee is educated about his company during the training period. He learns how the company functions, who holds the upper level positions, and what he has to do to someday become a wise and respected manager totally dedicated to his people and company.

Decision Making

The *ringi seido* or consensus in decision making is the style in Japan and is used by over 90% of the large firms, as well as many small and medium-sized firms.

All decisions are thoroughly reviewed and discussed by each relevant department that might be affected. A form, called the *ringi-sho* is circulated for the appropriate seal of approval. Reluctant persons will be allowed to question the initiator, which takes time and patience, as explanations and agreements may have to be repeated for each new group. The Japanese refer to this system as "bottom up" planning. While the reviewing process may take a lot of time from a Western perspective, once consensus is reached the implementation state is rapid and efficient.

Understanding the ringi is crucial to successful negotiations in Japan because it is the "filter" through which a Japanese negotiator's idea must pass. The negotiator may not have the authority to make decisions beyond those granted by the group. It is not uncommon for what could be a two-day negotiation session in the United States to last more than two weeks in Japan— in fact, it may be months before negotiations are completed.

While the use of the *ringi-sho* is widespread, it is not used for every transaction. A company will usually set a financial limit above which a *ringi-sho* is required but below which approvals for business decisions can be made by various individuals within the organization. For example, using dollar amounts, a *ringi-sho* is usually required for amounts over U.S.$1,000,000, with the general manager of a division able to approve transactions up to that amount. Within a division, transactions less than $500,000 may be approved by the manager or department head. These figures are examples of how the approval process may work, with the actual amounts varying between companies. What is important to note is that decision-making can be accomplished very quickly in many instances. The exception to this approval process is when the transaction involves advance payment or a high-risk investment.

Often, it is not the inability to make the decision that causes delays, but whether the individual has the responsibility for making the decision. This question of responsibility occurs as the Japanese employees interact in their daily work, making it difficult to draw clear lines of authority. Now, in many Japanese organizations individual decision making is encouraged and looked upon favorably by the employer who does not feel that it is necessary for an employee to always be reporting to one's boss.

According to Edward C. Stewart in *American Cultural Patterns; A Cross-Cultural Perspective,*

> 'The Confucian ethic, which still governs Japan, demands unanimity, and in order to respect the rights of the minority, the majority will compromise on almost every issue until a consensus of some kind is reached . . . No one must ever be completely defeated, because if he is, he cannot 'hold up his face.'"

In summary, Japanese businessmen seem to take a long time to make decisions. However, once they reach a decision, it is executed rapidly and completely. In addition, they react slowly to a need for a change in plans. The following is an example of how decision making takes place step-by-step when a Japanese company is going to purchase a large computer system:

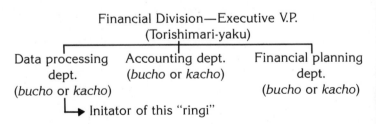

Financial Division—Executive V.P.
(Torishimari-yaku)

Data processing dept. (*bucho* or *kacho*)   Accounting dept. (*bucho* or *kacho*)   Financial planning dept. (*bucho* or *kacho*)

Initiator of this "ringi"

1. The initiator of the idea is a coordinator.

2. He discusses the idea with each relevant department.

3. He also receives agreement of the division vice-president. This decision is made at the financial division meeting, which is held every two weeks.

4. If someone opposes this issue, he discusses it with the coordinator during working hours or after working hours (called *nemawashi*).

5. Next, the coordinator must get an agreement from relevant departments such as: procurement, personnel, general council, maintenance, marketing, etc. (also involves *nemawashi*).

6. All decisions are thoroughly reviewed and discussed at the *bucho-kai* (department head meeting) once a month.

7. Then, a *ringi-sho* is issued.

8. The coordinator presents and answers any questions at *torishimari-yaku kai* or *jomu-kai* (executive V.P. meeting) once a month. Each executive V.P. was informed of this issue by their *bucho* before attending the meeting.

9. At this point, all decisions have been made.

10. The circulation of *ringi-sho* does not take a lot of time.

11. Depending on the subject (title of *ringi-sho*), the decision can be made at various levels (e.g., it may not be necessary to have the president's seal. This depends on the cost of the product to be purchased—usually, if the amount is more than $1 million the president's seal is required, but for less than $1 million the executive vice-president's seal is sufficient.

In reality, the *ringi-sho* is just *tatemae,* i.e., paper work. What takes time is the *nemawashi.* Below is a sample *ringi-sho.*

<u>Ringi-sho</u>   No._____

                         Date:_____

President   V.P.   Exec. V.P.
_____

_____

Department Managers:
    Personnel   Accounting   General
_____

_____

<u>Request for Approval</u>

            By: Y. Yamada, Bucho
                Data Processing Division
                        or
            By: Exec. Vice-President of
                Financial Division

1. Purchasing a Large Computer System
2. Product: ABC Computer
3. Amount: $1.5M
4. Reason: _____
           _____

Contrast of Decision-Making Systems

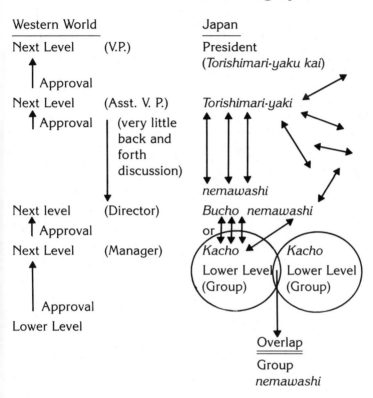

Western World

Next Level   (V.P.)

↑ Approval

Next Level   (Asst. V. P.)
↑ Approval | (very little back and forth discussion)

Next level   (Director)
↑ Approval

Next Level   (Manager)

↑

Approval

Lower Level

Japan

President
(*Torishimari-yaku kai*)

Torishimari-yaki

nemawashi

Bucho nemawashi
or
Kacho   *Kacho*
Lower Level   Lower Level
(Group)   (Group)

Overlap
Group
nemawashi

Conclusion:

Decisions made quickly, but implementation is slow and often ineffective.

Conclusion:

Decisions can take 2 weeks or 2 months, but once made, the implementation is generally smooth and effective.

Japanese Business Negotiating Courtesies

Protocol is scrupulously observed in Japan. The Japanese show deference and respect for others and express gratefulness for favors or special attention. Failure to do so may easily result in canceled negotiations.

The Japanese use extremely complex and ritualized forms of greetings and good-byes. The level of formality depends on the situation and persons involved. Nowadays in business situations, people use the standing bow, often together with a handshake, while saying their greetings and good-byes. The degree of the bow is determined by the overall formality and the status of the persons. All meetings open and close with some formality.

Third parties or intermediaries are often used for introductions and negotiations, and problems can be discussed with this person who can smooth things out behind the scenes.

Most Japanese businessmen have business cards printed in Japanese on one side and English on the other side. A Japanese businessman is rarely called by his first name; even close friends in Japan use the last name. Persons are usually referred to by their titles instead of their name, such as *kacho-san,* which means department head.

Japanese are punctual. Guests are typically attended to by a junior person for awhile and then an executive. Generally, guests are shown into a quiet, tastefully decorated lounge and served Japanese tea, coffee, or juice. Japanese rise when another member enters the room to be introduced, especially a senior who may very well come in later.

Styles of Communication

In Japan politeness is a must at all times. There is no separate business communication style, and formal good manners are the rule for all occasions. However, three levels of formality can be found. The highest level of politeness is maintained between important strangers (such as first business meetings) or when one desires to show extreme respect. A slightly less formal politeness is used for daily interactions between peers or once negotiations have begun. The least strict formality would be found among friends. It is important to be extremely sensitive to these levels of formality and to respond in kind.

Maintaining face—or self-respect—is crucial and negative responses are avoided at all costs. Japanese prefer to talk around an issue, since getting straight to the point might involve some confrontation.

For a Japanese, it is rude or impolite to interrupt an authority figure, such as a teacher or one's superior. A person's words are not separate from the person who has spoken them, and so to question the meaning of what someone has said appears to question the position of the person.

Everyone in Japan is connected. No one can conduct business without the help of many other people. These relationships are ongoing and deserve recognition at regular intervals as well as immediately after anything special. Personal relations are a fundamental basis to all Japanese transactions. Business is frequently introduced over tea, sake, or a game of golf. This is a time of evaluating each individual's strengths and weaknesses.

Japanese businessmen find out about each other by frequently taking clients out for a drink and dinner to a variety of entertainment spots. As time goes on, sports events or music concerts may be on the agenda as the Japanese discover the client's interests.

It is customary for employee groups to enjoy a variety of activities together. Most companies sponsor several annual events, like New Year's parties or picnics for families to enjoy together. Other activities are for company or department members only—without spouses.

The senior member or department head is expected to gather subordinates together and treat them to drinks and dinner on occasion. The senior member departs early and leaves behind some extra money. It is socially acceptable for anyone to say whatever they feel at these gatherings, including criticism of the boss and complaints about the company.

Entertaining is a large part of business in Japan. Both top and middle management entertain as the Japanese negotiator has a main goal of knowing in depth who he is working with. Wives generally do not accompany husbands on business/social occasions unless they are *specifically* invited to do so. This custom is strictly observed. Conversation over drinks is often the way to get to an informal level and "down to brass tacks," feelings that are difficult to achieve in the formal business meeting.

Although Japanese work long hours and come home late at night, they like to talk about hobbies, which can be anything from photography or mountain climbing to Chinese bronze study. Talking about hobbies allows people to get to know one another a little better on a personal basis without invading privacy. It also leads to discovery of common interests. From there, a discussion of sports, arts, music, Japan's progress, the company's achievements, new products, history, or famous people is acceptable.

Japanese Negotiating Principles

In negotiations, the Japanese strive for a "meeting of hearts" and Japanese negotiators are not solely concerned with the "bottom line" or end results. In other words, they evaluate the decision in terms of contributions to the good of the country or relationships within the company. The Japanese are concerned with achieving harmony and with "smoothing relationships" in order to reach a mutual goal.

During the discussions, the Japanese show flexibility in their positions with some modification between a first and second offer. However, the second offer is usually close to the first and is firm. What the Japanese have brought to the negotiating table are positions derived through consensus, so their offers and proposals are usually firm. During the negotiations the Japanese sometimes appear to be delaying, especially as the negotiations come to a close. This usually means one of three things: (1) taking time to deliberate a response to the question, (2) a desire not to answer, and (3) as a means to show the importance of the matter under discussion.

To facilitate negotiations in Japan, foreign negotiators should provide documents supporting any claims made concerning their product and company. Documents have a dual benefit. First, they provide written support for technical or other questions about the product or company; and second, they will support the decision to accept the business proposal. The second benefit provides the opportunity to "save face" in the event the venture is not a success, even though indigenous cultural aspects in the Japanese decision-making process prevent any one individual from receiving credit or blame for a decision regardless of its outcome.

The Japanese perception of time is much more subjective than it is for a Westerner. Time is important to the Japanese, but less so than to Westerners. Preliminary negotiations may be very prolonged while the atmosphere and issues are carefully assessed. Not being hasty is seen as a sign of wisdom and sincerity. Frequently top-level managers cannot be reached on short notice because they are so involved in meetings and human relations activities. Yet, the Japanese can also be incredibly efficient and aware of critical deadlines. Here they make no concession to subjective time. Neither are they prone to a lack of punctuality, which is considered impolite. If the negotiator is kept waiting for a long time, he can usually assume that his request has met with disfavor. A delayed response is generally the polite way for a Japanese to say "no."

Bound by strong cultural traditions, the Japanese make lifetime commitments. Once they have made the decision to engage in a selected business enterprise with a Westerner, the Japanese anticipate a long-lived involvement. With this in mind, the Japanese view negotiating with caution and proceed with care and concern. Because of this long-term attitude, the Japanese are concerned with getting to know the people and the company with whom they are dealing. They seek those with whom they can deal effectively and with whom there is mutual understanding and caring.

The Role of Government

Japan is governed through a centralized governmental system. In its trade policy, it has maintained a protective attitude toward local industry and displayed a tendency towards restricting imports. In recent years, this has slowly changed, such as the changes made in 1980 that now allow transactions with foreign exchange without the approval of the government, except in rare instances; whereas before 1980 advance approval was required in most cases. There also has been some loosening of the quota system since 1980, and the approval of the Ministry of Finance for international transactions is needed in fewer instances than in the past. It is highly recommended that an inquiry be made to the Ministry of International Trade and Industry (MITI) prior to entering the Japanese market. The Ministry will have information regarding protected industries, as well as the current restrictions and regulations regarding the items to be imported. The government also plays a role in the banking and insurance industries, with laws that fix interest rates and rates for life and marine insurance for instance.

Role of Attorneys

Attorneys in Japan are becoming increasingly important, especially within the last two to three years. Today, most large companies employ their own legal department. For example, the Mitsui Trading Company has a legal staff of approximately 50 specialists. All are not qualified as lawyers, but all have considerable knowledge of legal matters. Also, because of the complexity of international law and the need to be well versed, Mitsui sends two employees to Harvard Law School and two employees to Oxford for a two-year study in international law each year. The smaller companies will seldom employ their own lawyers but will have access to a law firm.

During negotiations in Japan the lawyer is rarely present, but the contract will be reviewed by the legal department, and in important and complex situations the ringi-sho will be passed through the legal division for comment and approval. In negotiations outside of Japan, due to the complexity of issues, it is common to bring a lawyer directly to the negotiating sessions.

Summary

The following is a summary of key points discussed in this chapter.

Selection Sytem — Lifetime Employment

- [ ] Rigid selection process—competition begins with quality of all schools attended.
- [ ] Ability to study is more important than intelligence level.
- [ ] Education is a continuing process even after college.
- [ ] Relative lack of creativity and originality in schools.
- [ ] Self-discipline, courtesy, and consideration is taught at home and at school.
- [ ] Education is geared to prepare persons to become exemplary workers.

Selection Process in Japanese Companies

- [ ] Servants to their company—loyalty and work of high quality and intensity is expected.
- [ ] Employees are helped to live better, feel satisfied, and be more productive, and are willing to advance in the company's structure.
- [ ] One's capacity to work well with others is important.
- [ ] A Japanese manager is more of a generalist than an American manager.
- [ ] Japanese negotiators will defer maximizing immediate profits to increase market share.
- [ ] Managers are promoted and salary increases are based on seniority in the company with consideration given to productiveness, morale, and cooperation.
- [ ] New employees are selected from top universities and must adapt to mentor system.
- [ ] Japanese companies are successful because of employees' feeling of belonging and believing their future success lies in the success of the company.

Training

☐ Graduates from a university work for a company knowing they will receive intensive company training.

☐ An employee must experience all steps in hierarchy to understand each employee's job.

☐ The company is a family away from home.

☐ Employees strive to learn from fellow workers and foreign visitors.

☐ It is important to learn how to listen carefully, absorb, then ask questions.

☐ A manager rarely displays knowledge and, in fact, may even underplay his understanding.

Japanese View of Negotiating Process

☐ Proceed with cautious, careful concern to establish long-term relationship.

☐ Seek people with whom they can deal effectively with mutual understanding.

☐ Make decisions by consensus.

☐ Must take place in harmonious atmosphere.

☐ Avoid direct conflict.

☐ Pre-discussions to conducting negotiations are crucial.

Decision Making

☐ Decisions are made from bottom up—*ringi.*

☐ After discussion at various levels, a written description of a proposed decision is prepared—*ringi sho.*

- [ ] The *ringi sho* is circulated to interested parties with discussions and changes.
- [ ] Seals of those concerned are placed on the document to indicate approval (no seal or an upside down seal indicates disapproval).
- [ ] Decisions are debated.
- [ ] Once a formal decision is made, implementation is quick and efficient.
- [ ] Patience is crucial on part of Westerner.
- [ ] Documents to support decision are essential.

This is the "cultural baggage" a Japanese negotiator brings to the table. Chapter 2 discusses his American counterpart.

2

Background and Values of U.S. Negotiators

*B*usiness in the United States is rapidly expanding into international business negotiations for two reasons: (1) in many products and industries, the United States has lost its competitive edge because of the significant relative advances in technology by foreign competitors—the label "Made in the U.S.A." is not as strong as it once was and the American negotiator must be more skillful; and (2) negotiation instead of confrontation or dominance (a method in colonial times) is a more viable alternative in working out relationships and business transactions.

> "It is so American (as a somewhat deflated King Kong is hoisted atop the Empire State Building). It is big. It is, if I may say, crazy. And it doesn't work."
>   Japanese Technician
>   Quoted in *Time*, December 26, 1983

This chapter is about the American negotiator and what he brings to the negotiating table. Common themes are identified and discussed so the American negotiator can better understand the cultural values and assumptions he relies on when he encounters his Japanese counterparts, how he might be perceived, and what areas of significant difference in values, styles, strategies might be in conflict with Japanese negotiators.

An Overview

The United States is a "low context" culture (concept developed by Edward T. Hall), and American negotiators generally use low context communications when negotiating with Japanese. This means most of the emphasis or search for understanding in the communication is placed in the spoken form, i.e., words. This results in Americans tending to see things in black or white terms and being uncomfortable with ambiguity, which causes many problems in Japan where subtle and circuitous approaches are necessary. For example, it is often best to begin negotiations with an informal explanation of the matter, a strategy that many Americans overlook. This allows the parties involved to understand each other's position without being forced to make public statements. Therefore, public disagreements and the losing of face by one or both sides is avoided. However, this informal process is time consuming and requires an understanding of the local cultural context. As the American executive seeks to avoid ambiguity, he will often press for clear-cut answers to specific questions, which will put him at a disadvantage in high context environments if he cannot accurately interpret his opponent's response.

Many American negotiators are also perceived by Japanese as being overly aggressive and pushy. Often the Americans seek fast reactions and decisions. This characteristic can be traced to several themes that make up American culture. Because competition is a characteristic in the American culture, aggressiveness is often praised and cultivated as a positive trait. Another factor that enhances this trait of aggressiveness is that motivation in American society is achievement oriented. Americans learn early they aren't worth much if they haven't "done" a lot.

Similarly, the American penchant for informality and quick "friendship" often causes the American negotiator to believe that good personal relations can often be more important than a good feasibility study. In Japan, relationships and friendships take a long time to grow. Instant friendships are "tasteless" and "shallow" for Japanese.

Because the performances of American businessmen are evaluated in terms of achievement, the American negotiator often tends to press for achieving short-term objectives and goals.

As a result, the American negotiator may avoid concessions so as to prove he is a good negotiator and thus further his own career goals. From the perspective of the company, this strategy is undesirable because concessions may be desirable to advance the organization's position. Further, a person who does not intend to concede any points often comes to the bargaining table with modest demands. This has an important effect on the outcome of negotiations as both parties' expectations are crucial variables in the negotiation process. Modest expectations often result in modest outcomes.

Frequently, American negotiators stop bargaining and settle for available terms because they are impatient. This has its roots in the fast pace of life in the U.S. and the notion that time is a commodity that is slipping by.

The American emphasis on specialization and professionalism also affects the negotiation process. An American negotiator may often become immersed in the narrow confines of his profession while ignoring the implications or the interests of the company as a whole. For example, an engineer may become so involved in the technical superiority of his product and ignore the need that the target market has for a simpler and scaled-down product. In this regard he may refuse to see the marketer's aim of giving the customer what he wants.

American negotiators tend to personalize their bargaining relationships. They are often surprised that an opponent may seem quite affable in a social context, but may exhibit quite a pugnacious behavior at the bargaining table.

American negotiators are expected to be competitive but they are also expected to be cooperative. This emphasis on cooperation leads Americans to believe that it is improper to be inflexible. In other words, they feel that concessions should be reciprocated. However, this perception of flexibility puts the Americans at a disadvantage if their opponent fails to perceive the benefits of flexibility. Therefore, if Americans make counter-demands that are refused, they tend not to continue to push them, because they feel that it might widen the range of conflict. However, they fail to see that counter-demands may actually facilitate agreement by giving them more flexibility in their own position.

American negotiators are also skillful in isolating conflicts and dealing with them. For example, within the framework of a problem that is woven into a fabric of commercial, financial, and military considerations, Americans are skillful in negotiating in one of these spheres without hurting their relationship in the others.

Because American law is a written law based on precedent, American negotiators emphasize contract terms to specify the rights and obligations of each party. However, Japanese also rely on the moral commitments and often become offended by the American negotiator's insistence on written details.

The Basis of the American Value System

As Graham and Herberger state in their *Harvard Business Review* article "Negotiators Abroad Don't Shoot from the Hip," engrained in the American way of life is the Protestant work ethic. It is seen as a product of our immigrant heritage that leads us to work hard and to accomplish our objectives. This pervasive theme has created the American sense of independence, individual achievement, and personal drive for success. As pioneers in a vast, unsettled land, time requirements for travel led to fewer negotiations, that out of necessity, were concise and time efficient. Today, we live in a mobile society where travel and communication can be accomplished with ease. Despite these changes, we continue to believe that one should effectively use one's time, since time is considered money, and this preoccupation with efficiency frequently jeopardizes our social relationships.

As *Time* magazine stated in its August 1983 special issue on Japan; the American civic principle is generally that of freedom and equality. We tend to value truth and honesty. Our socialization practices exemplify this commitment, as we believe that giving and taking feedback is a sign of strength and maturity. Candor is a respected American trait and is seen as an essential part of effective communication. Americans are known for their competitive spirit yet are simultaneously seen as extremely argumentative and impatient. Besides the desire to compete,

Americans generally see themselves as being constant and predictable. This is characterized by our desire to stick to our guns unless proven wrong.

Applying the American Value System to Negotiations

The following information was taken from John L. Graham's article "Brazilian, Japanese, and American Business Negotiations." It reveals a series of cultural factors that affect the outcome of American-Japanese negotiations.

Importance of Honesty

American bargaining strategies emphasize the exchange of information. The decision-making process at the bargaining table is extremely dependent upon this exchange. It was found that the probability of success is increased by encouraging the other team to speak about their particular bargaining position. The value placed on honesty is closely related to the issue of information exchange. Americans traditionally expect honesty and, as a result, are often victimized by the lack of clarity in their opponents' presentations. In a low-context culture, meaning and understanding are derived from what is verbally communicated.

Personal Relationships

In American business negotiations, the impression formed of one's opponents and their previous organizational experience is important. When attempting to enhance negotiation outcomes, negotiators do not spend enough time developing personal relationships with their opponents. When their bargaining opponents are seen as extroverted, younger, and less experienced, Japanese negotiators have difficulty in achieving positive outcomes at the bargaining table.

Selection Criteria

Glen Fisher in *International Negotiation: A Cross Cultural Perspective* indicates that in most U.S. corporations the individual with the greatest technical expertise is the one most frequently chosen to represent the interests of the company. This attitude is most prevalent when a product or product line is the subject of negotiations. The key to success is believed to be linked to product knowledge—its uses or how it functions, its strengths and weaknesses, its development and production. The belief is the more fluently the negotiator is able to discuss these issues, the better chance the negotiation has for obtaining satisfactory results.

Previous international experience is also a factor in selecting U.S. negotiators, although experience in the country or culture under consideration is not always a necessity. More important may be the length of time an individual has been working in the international department, even if the time has been spent negotiating with other countries. Justification for this type of selection process lies in the assumption that "after all, people are pretty much alike everywhere." If an individual has had successful negotiating experience with people from one country, these skills are viewed as transferable, and very little consideration is given to the different cultural bases of the people involved in the negotiations.

Another choice may be the individual who has successfully handled domestic negotiations. Experience with "negotiating a deal" and being able to obtain equitable yet profitable results for the company is viewed as the important skill. It is often believed that success domestically should ensure success internationally.

Assuming that technical expertise and previous experience are good predictors of international success also means that an individual's position within the corporation or division is an important factor in the selection process. This is brought out by Graham in his research concerning business negotiations in Brazil, Japan, and the United States. If a contract is at stake, the company is more likely to choose the person with the most experience and who has met with the most success in similar situations. The company will look to the negotiator who is persuasive, knowledgeable, and will represent the best interests of the company in order to obtain a profitable deal. The prospect of promotion may also come into play. Whether the individual accepts the position, and ultimately whether the negotiation is a success, may be a determining factor in the promotion process.

How They View the Negotiation Process

As the American style of negotiating is examined, it is important to explore the way in which Americans view the negotiation process. After the selection process is completed, "the chosen one," anticipates a trip to the bargaining table, and perhaps discusses the future meeting with his colleagues. The American view of the entire process begins to take shape, but specific strategies and processes necessary for effective bargaining are often overlooked. Sensing that a universal code of conduct exists precludes the use of different skills appropriate for each cultural/organizational context. Americans traditionally assume that their goals and objectives are shared by other countries. For example, Americans place much emphasis on efficiency in which the profitability of each transaction is of major concern. The best gauge of success is the extent to which short-term profits have been achieved.

Americans approach the entire negotiation process as a system, almost as if it were a game. Fisher stated that Americans generally see negotiating as similar to dealing with a series of problem-solving exercises. The negotiation session itself gives the American an opportunity to utilize his creative salesmanship—an opportunity to potentially "win." The negotiator, in his attempt to stay focused on strategy, separates the purpose or issue at hand from the people with whom he is negotiating. It is believed that this separation is essential for success in negotiating and that compromising on this position would undoubtedly result in unsatisfactory outcomes. These conflicting perspectives confuse Japanese negotiators, who see the issues being negotiated and the negotiators as the same, and makes it difficult for the Japanese to get a clear sense of their American counterparts.

How American Negotiators Are Trained

Both formal and informal training impacts the American's sense of his role in the negotiation process. According to Graham and Herberger, the educational system teaches Americans to compete in both academics and sports, and we are subsequently judged according to our ability to succeed in both of these arenas. Entering professional degree programs is a mere continuation of the emphasis on competition and the ultimate goal of "winning."

The studies of Graham and Herberger on American business and law schools suggest that students are not taught how to ask questions, how to get information, how to listen, nor how to relate to those with whom they work. Americans are forced to learn through mistakes; at times repeating these mistakes at the risk of damaging a personal or corporate image.

Generally, U.S. corporations have failed to provide the necessary tools for negotiators involved in international work. When U.S. corporations have sent their managers overseas to transact business directly with foreign clients, the American executive left the U.S. virtually tool-less, armed with only the expectation of performing well. Unfortunately, domestic know-how doesn't make one capable of conducting business in unfamiliar (foreign) contexts. The expectation that success could result under such circumstances was hardly well founded.

Negotiation: American Style

The American negotiator chosen by his company usually has full authority to develop and close a deal during the negotiation process. According to Fisher, when he meets the members of the other negotiating team, he has an immediate desire to know who their decision maker is. He wants to know his counterpart as soon as possible in an effort to begin sizing up the competition. When he discovers he may not have an exact counterpart on the other team or that the negotiators' authority to make decisions may be rather limited, the American finds himself in a very frustrating situation. He discovers that he not only must convince the members of the negotiating team that his position has value, and that this must be communicated to decision makers who are not present at the negotiations.

The American also comes to the bargaining table with a certain amount of flexibility and leeway in making the final decisions that will be acceptable to his company. In turn, he expects to find similar flexibility in his counterparts, and he maneuvers to find how much they are willing to compromise or how far from their stated position they are willing to move. The American is familiar with a "give a little, get a little" process and lacks understanding of what appears to be a one-position attitude of the Japanese. This causes confusion for the American negotiator and often leaves him with the feeling of wondering how to proceed. The Japanese negotiators, on the other hand, say they "give a little to get a little" but feel U.S. negotiators want to "give nothing and get something."

Components of the Final Agreement

Once all the facts and positions are known, the American is able to make a relatively quick decision. Johnson and Ouchi in their article "Made in America (Under Japanese Management)" discuss this approach to finalizing the agreement. The choices are considered, and the costs and benefits of each possibility are weighed. Then the final decision is made with conviction. The American strives for and prides himself in time efficiency in this aspect of the decision-making process. He expects that his opponents will follow the same procedure.

Making a decision is the final point for the American negotiator whether it is on one issue within the negotiations or at the close of the entire process. At this time he is particularly interested in striving for closure and clarifying all the issues at hand. He wants to know exactly where everything stands and wants no loose ends or loopholes that could later cause problems. There is no room for vagueness or open-ended statements that could be interpreted in more than one way.

In reaching and finalizing an agreement, the American negotiator signs a contract in the name of his company. He expects that the agreement will be honored by all parties involved. This is a legal document that cannot be changed unless mutually agreed. If a change is suggested after what the American considers to be the final agreement, he is confused and views it as an affront, not only to the agreement itself but also to his integrity as a negotiator.

Number of Negotiators

A typical American-Japanese negotiating session has fewer Americans than Japanese, which reflects far more than just an attitude toward an appropriate number of negotiators. Americans often view the business negotiation as a process that can be handled by one skilled and knowledgeable person. They take pride in being able to tackle a problem single-handedly, in knowing all the pertinent facts and being able to address any issue concerning the subject at hand.

The presence of several members on a Japanese negotiating team gives evidence to their differing attitude. Graham and Herberger outline several activities that are concurrently required of a negotiator during a negotiating session. While he is talking or listening, he must also be thinking up arguments, developing explanations, formulating his own questions, or deciding how he will proceed to reach an agreement. While the Japanese use a team system to divide these responsibilities, for the American negotiator the task may become somewhat burdensome. Though it may be more economical and at the same time boost one's ego to be able to handle all those responsibilities, it may be more efficient in the long run to use more than one mind to sort through all the issues at hand.

Graham and Herberger also state that the American negotiator likes to "lay his cards on the table" at the beginning of the negotiating session, and expects his opponent to do the same. In this manner each side can see exactly where the other stands. When the American can use his native language to accomplish this task, he definitely feels he has the upper hand. The preciseness of the English language provides the perfect means of stating issues directly, a quality the American admires, especially in business dealings. He expects this same directness from his opponents and is frustrated when it is absent. Language can also be used in a more aggressive manner in an effort to draw out the opponent, trying to push him to be more verbal or more direct.

Negotiation is a complex process. An effective way to understand this complexity is to separate the process into individual issues and settle them one at a time. In this manner each point can be thoroughly examined, a decision can be made, if appropriate, and then it can be put aside and the next issue addressed. This procedure allows the negotiator to concentrate his efforts in one area at a time, making a series of decisions as he negotiates.

What the American often does not understand is that in the Japanese culture *nothing* is settled until the final stage of the negotiation process. He may find himself in an awkward situation when he has successfully separated the issues but cannot seem to prompt his opponent to make a definite decision on any of them.

The American also values persistence and strives for closure whether it is on an individual point or the final stage of the process. The American negotiator may continue to strive for decisions, using threats or warnings in an effort to achieve that end. Unfortunately, this strategy may serve to alienate the opponent and is more likely to lead to continued indecision or possibly a firm negative response.

The use of such pressure reveals a specific attitude of many American negotiators. As discussed by John Ilich in *The Art and Skill of Successful Negotiation,* the negotiation process is viewed as being similar to a "combat" situation. The other party is an "opponent." The way to get what you want is to "attack" and be persistent. A successful negotiation is a "battle" or a "war" that has been "won." Reference is made to the combat strategies of General George S. Patton in relation to the negotiation strategies of the American businessman. "The way to prevent the enemy from attacking you is to attack him and keep right on attacking him. This prevents him from getting set." This attitude has provided the background and foundation for many of the current strategies being applied by U.S. negotiators.

The most recent developments in strategies employed see a softening of the warlike attitude, though its presence is still evident. Most lecturers and negotiation seminar leaders now promote negotiations that result in a "win-win" situation. The basic aim is to reach an agreement that benefits all parties. The interests of each must be kept in mind and met throughout the negotiation process. The 1981 Harvard Negotiation Project of Fisher and Ury also recommends "principled negotiation" focusing on "mutual gains" and "just outcomes."

The key in these new strategy developments is their emphasis on the process as well as the outcome. An important element in the process is the negotiators themselves, their cultural background, and the attitudes they bring with them to the negotiating table.

Protocol—Does It Exist?

In one respect the American expects the Japanese to be flexible, to adopt a bargaining stance, and to be willing to make concessions and compromise in an effort to reach a point of mutual satisfaction. However, to take on an intense "bargaining" attitude during negotiations is in conflict with Japanese protocol. To the Japanese it is more important to be constant and firm during the negotiation process, stating the interests of the company clearly and not vacillating from one position to another.

On the other hand, *once an agreement is reached,* it is the American who is inflexible and uncompromising. The American negotiator assumes that contracts should be honored as initially stated. To the Japanese, once an agreement is reached, it is not unethical but rather most reasonable to consider changes that may lead to a more desirable agreement, especially if there is a change in circumstances.

When the American enters the negotiating situation, he immediately tries to determine the best English speaker among the Japanese. Once the American identifies this person, an assumption is frequently made that this individual is also the smartest and most influential member of the group. The American's efforts are then concentrated on this individual. The majority of questions and comments may be directed to him. This scenario, in fact, may create discomfort or cause anxiety for the individual involved, as well as offend the other members of the negotiating team. Among Japanese negotiators, expertise is more often a shared responsibility rather than being concentrated in one individual as is most frequent among American negotiators. To not address a question or comment to the appropriate individual on the Japanese negotiating team may be the beginning of more serious communication difficulties between the negotiating teams.

Americans also prefer a more relaxed atmosphere at the negotiating table than do their Japanese counterparts. Protocol is downplayed, an example of which is the Americans' quickness to encourage the use of first names. This effort to put everyone at ease may merely result in increased tension, as the Japanese place importance in observing formality and addressing individuals with their proper titles or surnames.

Americans also feel comfortable using casual social gatherings as occasions to conduct business. The American negotiator views this as an opportunity to explain his point of view in a more relaxed atmosphere, hoping to find his opponent in the same relaxed frame of mind. To the Japanese, the social occasion is also an integral part of business life but *detailed* discussions of business are usually reserved for the business day. When negotiations are going well, social occasions are often used to consolidate agreements. When the negotiations are going poorly, business discussions during a social occasion are perceived by the Japanese as inappropriate and in bad taste.

Concluding Comments and Some Advice

☐ Researchers and negotiators alike have documented the difficulty associated with international negotiations. Problematic areas continue to arise by virtue of the opposing cultural perspectives of the parties involved.

☐ It is imperative that American negotiators develop an awareness of their own cultural background in addition to that of our opponents.

☐ As we begin to integrate our knowledge of both cultural perspectives, we increase the possibility of success in international negotiations (a win-win situation).

☐ To negotiate successfully in Japan, the American must not only learn to accomplish the task, but he must also develop positive interpersonal relationships with his Japanese counterparts.

☐ American negotiators should also learn to develop several alternative courses of action in the event one fails. And to choose the one that will work best in Japan.

The next chapter discusses in more detail how Japanese negotiators perceive their American counterparts.

3

How Japanese Perceive American Negotiators

Walter Lippman, the well-known American writer, called "the pictures in our heads" of groups of people whom we don't know stereotypes. He stated that stereotypes are exaggerations of reality but are frequently accepted as fact.

Are stereotypes accurate? Some are, but the majority are not. Do they cause prejudice? Sometimes, but more frequently they reinforce existing opinions and viewpoints. The premise of this chapter is that it is useful to know some of the "stereotypes" Japanese negotiators may hold of American negotiators.

The material in the left column of the following pages is taken verbatim from a paper entitled "Negotiating with Americans." The material was purportedly written by a Japanese business-man [who did not attach his name to the document] and was for the benefit of Japanese negotiators. It is included here to give American negotiators a flavor of some of the things they may say about us, "behind our backs." In the middle of the page is a brief analysis of the salient points for negotiators in the document, and on the right are some implications for American negotiators.

Analysis of and Implications for American Negotiators

Negotiating with the Americans*	Analysis	Implications for American Negotiators
Introduction At the start I must apologize for stating my ideas on this subject so boldly when my superiors already know more than I about the subject. I have had more than five years' experience in dealing with U.S. negotiators and in all modesty report my findings in the hope that others can benefit. The subject deserves high evaluation and many hours of intense study so that we understand better our American friends.	Japanese often begin speeches or papers with an apology.	Be humble about your accomplishments. "A mature rice plant bends in the world" —Japanese proverb

* Author unknown. The document was received by this writer from someone at the United States Information Agency who is unsure of the origin. However, the perceptions described here are consistent with those expressed by many Japanese negotiators.

Background

U.S. negotiators are difficult to understand because they come from a background of different nationalities and experiences. Unlike Japanese the Americans are not racially or culturally homogeneous. Even their way of speaking English varies. Gaining a good understanding of one U.S. representative is only a little help in understanding others. Americans from large cities are different from those coming from small towns. There are differences between east and west, north and south, as well as in religion and national origin. Thus much of what they do is truly unpredictable and erratic. At the same time there is reason to suspect that beneath the rather disorderly appearance of U.S. negotiating teams whose members

Japanese may expect us to behave similarly to other Americans they have known.

This author suggests each one is different. The behavior of American negotiators is unpredictable (but, from a Japanese perspective, perhaps this is deliberate and a negotiating strategy).

U.S. negotiators appear disorganized, uncaring for each other and not unified.

Be consistent in presenting your position, and plan your strategy so that each member of your team is fully versed in the issues to be discussed.

Special efforts should be made to be well-organized, well-aware of each team member's stand on the issues and work together as a team.

Listen, listen
Listen, listen

(continued on next page)

Negotiating with the Americans*

often seem not to be listening to each other and who may not even dress in the same style, there is a calculated set of tactics and objectives which guide them. Sometimes U.S. representatives seem to make mistakes or to be ignorant of commonly known facts, but their lack of humility in such cases may mean that they really know what they are doing.

The background of American history is an important influence on their attitudes. The American frontier was a major factor from the arrival of the first settlers from Europe and for about 250 years. American books describe how the west was conquered or won. In some

Analysis

U.S. negotiators argue and may be confrontational.

There is order and harmony in the world.

Implications for American Negotiators

Do not cause your colleagues or negotiating counterparts to "lose face" in public.

Present a total picture in which everything is interrelated. The Japanese need to see the forest *and* the trees.

strange way the empty spaces of America had to be captured from nature which was like an enemy. This is a complete contrast to our idea that one must live in harmony with nature.

Americans also highly evaluate what they call adversary proceedings. This seems to come from their court system where two sides argue their cases in a direct confrontation with no effort made to find any harmony at all. Then the judge issues a ruling one way or the other without private consultation with the two sides and with no value given to conciliating the feelings of those in the case. Americans believe this undemocratic system is the best way to learn the truth and impose justice.

Japanese do not find direct confrontation and arguing a valuable method of negotiating.

Harmony and the feelings of others are of utmost importance in negotiations.

When disagreements arise, direct confrontations are to be avoided. Do not cause any member of either side to become embarrassed or lose face.

(continued on next page)

Negotiating with the Americans*	Analysis	Implications for American Negotiators
Americans sometimes say "truth is relative," or that "there is no such thing as black and white, only shades of grey," but often they act differently. They are seekers of truth and morality, just as we are, but they think truth and morality exist apart from the practical world around them. So in a negotiation it is common for American negotiators to say what basic principles are important. Later they may reject a sound practical idea because it violates principle. Therefore, it is necessary to be cautious about agreeing to any statement of principles and always point out the need for workable understandings. One possibility is that their fixed	Americans approach things in either/or, right/wrong, black/white terms. Getting things "on paper" may not have the same meaning attached to it for Japanese as it does for Americans.	Realize that Japanese principles and interpretation of truth and morality may be different from Americans'. Strive for workable mutual understandings of these basic concepts. Contracts and relationships can change and reinterpretation may be necessary if the circumstances change.

ideas about truth come from Christian religion which promises perfection at some future time or after death, so many American negotiators try to negotiate perfect and final agreements which they think will never need reinterpretation or adjustment. Indeed, once an agreement is signed they may be very rigid about it because they think it is perfect. As to Christianity, I am not sure what it teaches because there are many different kinds of Christians.

Americans have had a world leadership role since the end of World War II. They understand and are proud of their status, but seem not to know how they got there. They often talk about how hard we Japanese work, but many Americans work hard and they can be extremely

Americans appeared to be narrow-minded, egotistical, naive and wasteful. The American viewpoint may be "America *is* #1. "This is different from the viewpoint "Japan *as* #1."

Americans need to demonstrate flexibility, openness to new ideas, greater understanding and appreciation for own culture and other culture.

(continued on next page)

| | **Implications for American Negotiators** |
| **Negotiating with the Americans*** | **Analysis** |

clever sometimes. However, they seem to attribute their leadership status not to hard work but to the idea that they know the truth and are moral. Thus they are convinced that their ideas are right and others must follow or reveal themselves as fools or knaves. This may seem a harsh judgment, and it is overstated, but Americans are often ethnocentric without knowing it. Americans also take as given the tremendous wealth of their country, including rich deposits of minerals and petroleum as well as agricultural land. They waste these resources as if there were no end to them, spreading out over the land inefficiently and seeming not to notice.

U.S. Negotiating Preparations

Without access to their secrets I can only guess, from their behavior and what they tell me, how the Americans prepare for negotiations. They have procedures much like ours, but sometimes seem not to follow them. Often they argue even more in private. This is part of their idea of adversary proceedings, and they seem to feel no shame about such embarassing behavior.	Americans lack sensitivity to Japanese behavior and what is acceptable.	Do not argue during negotiations—prepare your positions in advance.
The procedures they use include careful study of the Japanese position, the reasons for it, and the negotiating pressure each side can apply. They spend the most time on their own position. Like the Japanese government they have many different agencies with different interests which must be recon-	American negotiators do not spend sufficient time understanding the Japanese position.	*Listen*

(continued on next page)

Negotiating with the Americans*	Analysis	Implications for American Negotiators
ciled. This is done by circulating draft papers and holding meetings at which middle level officials discuss what to do. Each of these officials represents his own superiors and has limited power to express his own ideas, unlike Japanese officials at that level whose advice is usually accepted since they have more time to study and become experts on detailed matters.		
U.S. Negotiating Procedures		
U.S. negotiators often have fall-back positions which they can use if they do not win agreement to first proposals. These fall-backs are worked out in ad-	Japanese may have a lack of trust of Americans' positions because they change so frequently.	Spend more efforts on commonalities. Prepare a position with a small upper and lower range. Be able to support this position.

vance almost as if they knew their first offers were unreasonable. They do not prepare one approach as the best under the circumstances, while giving their negotiators authority to approach the matter flexibly. Therefore it is necessary for us to learn what the final fall back is as early as possible. Once that information is obtained it is often possible to get the U.S. side to offer its fall-back proposal in return for a concession of no consequence.

The Americans also try to predict what our reactions will be. They prepare contingency plans which they hope will counter our arguments, again believing that confrontation and rebuttal are necessary. They seem to value highly winning such arguments. When arguments do develop U.S. nego-

Japanese want to understand the whole picture.

Japanese are traditionally formal and polite and will keep emotions to themselves. Will cover up their feelings and not express them.

American humor is difficult to understand for Japanese since it is mostly based on our cultural experiences.

Japanese often lose trust in those who make "unreasonable" offers.

Present what is a viable fair proposal and work to adjust it to benefit both parties. Americans should make every effort to maintain a calm, even, and consistent behavior throughout all negotiations.

Humor and jokes are culturally conditioned. Be aware of this,

(continued on next page)

Negotiating with the Americans*	Analysis	Implications for American Negotiators
tiators may become tense, after which they may try to distract attention from a difficult situation by resorting to humor. Their humor is hard to understand since it is based on their own rather strange cultural experience, but it is safe to laugh when they do.		and if "telling jokes" is a style, be cautious. Japanese may laugh to be polite, but may not understand the joke.

In the Negotiating Room

	Analysis	Implications for American Negotiators
U.S. negotiating teams are sometimes small and sometimes large. Their delegations are often large when the internal disagreements between agencies have not been reconciled before the meeting, and therefore, each department (or sub-department) must send an agent. On the other hand, they	Japanese spirit of unity and free press permits some public knowledge of the negotiations' progress.	Be prepared for possible observers.

often limit the number on their side, perhaps because of internal jealousy. They do not always admit observers from interested agencies and seldom have anyone present for training purposes or as an extra notetaker. Thus our delegation is usually larger. Americans are not used to having cameramen in the meeting room and may be surprised when they encounter a large group of photographers when they arrive. Secretly however, they seem to like the show as if it were a kind of flattery, and not just the curiosity of our press representatives who compete so hard with each other.	
Americans are quite conscious of protocol, so it is necessary to consider seating and the matter of introductions and entertainment. They often say that rank means nothing to them, but it	Americans are rank and status conscious Japanese may use social events to gain information on possible counter-proposals.	Give information on social occasions if you think that it is appropriate.

(continued on next page)

Negotiating with the Americans*

really does. On the other hand, when mistakes are made they adapt easily and are not offended if the matter is quietly corrected. In short, they want the proper gestures made but are satisfied with that. They also like to be invited to social events where they say they dislike discussing business and then in fact easily agree to do so. Such occasions are useful for testing compromises and obtaining information on their fall back positions.

The Progress of Talks

Americans are energetic and persistent. They are enthusiastic negotiators who seldom take naps during talks even if

Analysis

Japanese may not show they are paying attention the same way Americans do. Japanese may even take a short "nap"

Implications for American Negotiators

Be prepared to allow for sufficient time for negotiations. Americans rush through things where the Japanese would the topic is of no real concern. They enjoy arguing the logic of their position which they like to describe as good for all and not just for them. They have a disturbing habit, however, of passing over very quickly the areas of agreement and giving high emphasis to disagreements. In fact, they talk about little else, as if that were the most important subject!

Americans like to concentrate on one problem at a time. They seem not to understand that the whole picture is more important, and they spend little time on developing a general understanding of the views and interests of both sides. Since their habit of focusing on one issue often forces a direct disagreement they often propose setting the issue aside, but then they come back to it later with the same attitude and concentra-

during important negotiations. Japanese negotiators spend a lot of time reviewing areas of agreement.

Japanese need to understand a complete picture and not just the parts. If you can't draw the whole picture a Japanese feels uncomfortable and doesn't want to get into detail. On the other hand, Japanese are sometimes very nit-picky and want to discuss every detail. During discussions, a Japanese businessman is drawing the whole picture again and again to ensure the detail will not destroy the whole picture.

rather work calmly, slowly— taking time to get to know the other party and establish a good relationship in order to work together harmoniously.

Do not dismiss areas of agreement and focus on disagreements. Return to areas of agreement as this will build a strong relationship.

Make sure to focus on issue as a whole and the common benefits to both parties rather than dwell on points of disagreement.

(continued on next page)

Negotiating with the Americans*

Analysis

Implications for American Negotiators

tion. A negotiation with them may therefore become a series of small conflicts, and we must always make a special effort to give proper attention to the large areas of agreement and common interests.

During negotiations the Americans sometimes forget that we are frequently called upon to brief the press and that events in the talks may be fully described in our newspapers. It is necessary to explain to them that this is our idea of how a free press works and that unattributed reports on the progress of negotiations are useful to prepare the public for the final results. It is helpful to discuss with them in advance the sub-

This doesn't generally apply to business negotiations but rather to government-to-government negotiations.

jects which can be described to the press. Usually they will then agree to general briefing, but if this is not done they may complain about reports they did not expect to see in the newspapers. When our press people force us to say more than we had agreed we would say, the Americans profess to be quite disturbed.

When talks are concluded the U.S. side always feels some kind of euphoria. They like to think they have won, which is part of the adversary style common to them. They may engage in some public gloating to justify themselves to their countrymen. This is annoying when they do, but I suppose we should try to understand such behavior and recognize that they really cannot help themselves and do not mean any harm.

> Americans try to "win" . . . to get the best deal . . . even to the detriment of the Japanese side.

> Coming to a negotiated agreement is a mutual benefit to both parties. One party did not win over the other. Long term relationships will continue and improve if the terms are mutually beneficial.

It is useful to know what ideas Japanese negotiators may have of us. This knowledge may help explain why they act and react the way they do . . . especially when we are negotiating with them.

The implications for American negotiators suggest some behavioral guidelines which, if they become part of the repertoire of our behaviors, will result in more positive perceptions of us on the part of our Japanese counterparts. And this should lead to more successful business negotiations.

The remaining parts of this chapter provide additional background on Japanese negotiators in an attempt to help U.S. negotiators understand why they think and behave the way they do. For those who are well versed in "things Japanese," I recommend skipping to Chapter 4.

Japan's Past

The exact origin of the Japanese people is unknown, but it is believed they have inhabited their four major islands plus many of the smaller ones for at least 6,000 years. Early Japanese culture was influenced by Buddhist missionaries from China, who contributed to many of the basic assumptions about life. This tradition valued external order and harmony within the society. It also emphasized the collective aspect of the social order.

Prior to the Meiji Restoration in 1868, Japan was isolated for more than 250 years. The social and business system in Japan today is based upon dependency, loyalty, strong group cohesion, and family ties. The overall goal for Japanese, in the present as in the past, in their activities is harmony with people and nature.

Japanese society is homogeneous, and being Japanese means that one is somehow part of an extended family.

For centuries Japanese society has been founded upon extended patriarchal family patterns. Authority, deriving from a senior male member, flowed down through male heads of related households to form a clan structure. During the medieval years of civil wars and political chaos, the family clan served as the principal physical and psychological support of the individual.

Two characteristics of Japanese society, *ie* and *amae,* later to play vital roles in the corporate culture, were developed during this period. Ie is the family model imposed upon extra-familial relationships. It is a feature of male dominance, female submission, and a general respect for the elderly that has been transferred to many Japanese institutions. *Amae* is the desire for security. In a broader sense it also involves the sublimination of self-interest for the security and protection of the group. It is through the learning of *amae* that Japanese society has become deeply group-conscious, constantly striving for the ideals of harmony and unanimity.

As the constant internal warfare of innumerable power struggles subsided, some members of the *samurai* (warrior caste) found less violent roles as administrators for various warlords. Eventually, these functionaries and their families were accorded titles of nobility, and thus a feudal society of gentry and peasantry was born.

During the Tokugawa Shogunate of the sixteenth century, internal commerce evolved sufficiently to also allow for a lucrative trade with China and Korea. Members of the *samurai* class began to assume new importance as business entrepreneurs, largely at the expense of many previously independent village traders. The expansion of *samurai* enterprises was greatly eased by the existent feudal relationship of lord and master, a social model also followed within many Japanese institutions.

During the Meiji Era of the nineteenth century, which finally opened Japan to the Western world, the *samurai* class was often the first adopters of Western innovations. *Samurai* family enterprises developed rapidly into major business cartels known as *zaibatsu.* These family cartels were officially disallowed at the end of World War II but in fact remain powerful influences in Japanese commerce.

The introduction of Western concepts of business and economics did not cause great social dislocations, but did fit into Japanese familial models. All levels of the former society—the *samurai,* farmers, workers, and merchants—began to recognize and find meaning in the obligations of their positions to the family firm or to the nation. In this receptive climate the familial drives of *ie* and *amae* were easily transplanted in the *zaibatsu* organizational structure. Management took a paternalistic approach towards personnel relations: adopting valued employees, selecting marriage partners, and inculcating the concepts of thriftiness and education. The skilled male worker was rewarded with the security of lifetime employment, and promotion was based upon seniority within the organization.

Aspects of Japanese Management Behavior

There exists in the upper strata of Japanese management an informal association of top executives known in Japanese as *zaikai.* Close interpersonal relationships and the economic and political power which the zaikai share have earned them the epithet "Japan, Inc."

The prestige of a member of the zaikai can often be measured by the extent of his *jinmyaku* (personal connections). Jinmyaku can assume various forms, but most obvious are those connections cultivated through industry organizations. Four of the principal organizations through which the *zaikai* interact are:

- □ *Keidanren* (Federation of Economic Organizations)—in 1981, it comprised 110 powerful industry associations orchestrating the production policy of iron and steel, vehicles, ship-building, petrochemicals, electronics, and electrical power.
- □ *Nikkeiren* (Japan Federation of Employers' Associations)—advises labor negotiation for 54 industry organizations, reflecting 29,000 individual companies and 10 million workers (1981 figures).
- □ *Keizai Doyukai* (Japan Committee for Economic Development)—conducts discussions of national policy for some 1,000 influential managers on the rise.
- □ *Nissho* (Japan Chamber of Commerce and Industry)—the oldest but least influential of the four since it primarily projects the interests of small and medium-sized companies (Dahlby 1981).

Apart from relations developed through industry associations there are other types of jinmyaku as well. *Keibatsu* (extended family connections) are very important, as might be expected given the familial nature of Japanese business. It is reputed that family connections even play instrumental roles in the election of prime ministers.

Gakubatsu (university connections) are equally strong. (Mitsukoshi, the largest department store in Japan, recruited 80% of its management team from Keio University.) In recent years a third of the House of Representatives of the Diet and over a third of the *zaikai* have been graduates of Tokyo University. Other schools of high status are the National universities of Kyoto, Tohoku, Nagoya, Hokkaido, and Fukuoka and the elite private schools of Keio, and Waseda. The Tokyo "Ivy League" schools now include, Tokyo, Keio, Waseda, Meiji, Hosei, and Rikkyo.

Participation in political interest groups creates a type of jinmyaku known as *seikai*. Political interest connections can be formed through active membership in political parties, lobbying groups, or the Keizai Doyukai or one of the committees of the Keidanren whose influence of opinion is considerable.

A more direct type of political jinmyaku are the *kinmyaku* (money connections). These are relationships based upon the *zaikai's* financial contribution to politicians. In a broader sense *kinmyaku* encompasses the communality of shared educational and family backgrounds, as well as reflecting the practice of business executives "retiring" into politics or governmental service.

Japanese commerce, then, can be viewed as a tapestry of interpersonal business connections, held together by the trust and intimacy of shared obligations and expectations. *Amakudari* is the appointment of a former government official to a responsible position in a private company. This is possible because government officials generally retire at 55 years of age and most executives of private companies don't retire until age 60 or 65.

Japanese Workers

Many Westerners retain a false image of the Japanese worker as an "economic animal"—living to work, satisfied with low pay and long hours, and unreasonably loyal to a management that blatantly exploits and abuses him. This image is incorrect. It has been shown in various studies that Japanese workers are as dissatisfied as Westerners with production line work.

That a particular task is boring and simplistic is well appreciated by the Japanese worker, but his acceptance of a job situation rests upon other criteria. The social interaction of small groups designed for workers within the corporate family has fulfilled a greater desire of Japanese workers than the need for interesting work. By participating in company-sponsored social clubs, sports, or recreational activities and by sharing the living arrangements of company dorms and housing, the worker can satisfy the need to belong, *amae*, and strengthen his identification as a member of the extended family. Robert J. Ballon in *The Japanese Employee* writes:

> "In the eyes of the Japanese, it is not the occupation *(shokugyo)* that counts, but the place of work *(shokuba)*. In other words, it is not what a man does that is the important industrial dimension, but where he does it. It has been pointed out that when a child is asked, "What does your father do?" the answer in the West is usually given in terms of the father's occupation, whereas in Japan it is given in terms of the company that employs the father."

Company identification as opposed to task identification is also promoted through quality control circles and the practice of job rotation.

The fact that there is a low level of task orientation among blue-collar workers has influenced the structure of labor unions. "Enterprise unions," in which membership is undifferentiated by jobs or skills and to which all company employees belong, have been the norm (except for managers above *kacho*, who cannot be union members). Membership in unions is somewhat inconsequential as an interpersonal mechanism. Workers tend to approach union involvement submissively. Open labor disputes are usually limited to issues of pay, while the less frequent negotiations regarding work conditions occur on higher executive levels. Normally, there is cooperation and collaboration between unions and management in Japan.

Hierarchical Relations

Much of Japanese business is founded upon the concepts of *ie* and *amae*. That is, management prefers a paternalistic style and employees value job security and corporate identification.

Authority, as a psychological feature of hierarchical relations, involves great risk. For the Japanese an authoritative situation is extremely emotional and personal; it engenders great psychological meaning. The power of a supervisor over a subordinate is viewed as a threat to harmonious relations; it implies a conflict. On the other hand, authority is also compelling for its offer of security. To reduce the direct confrontation of command the Japanese employee has sought to personalize authority by establishing a close relationship with the supervisor. In executing an order the employee strives mightily to please, quickly and efficiently, and the supervisor acknowledges the effort with expressions of his personal concern for the employee. Also, orders are analyzed, questioned, and the best method of approach sought by the employee to participate, in some small way, in the formulation of the order, thereby muting its confrontational nature.

Ambition also functions as an ambivalent element of vertical relations. The desire for advancement is strong throughout Japanese business, but it is seldom expressed. The disruption of seniority-based promotion and the competition that advancement implies are inconsistent with the ideal of social harmony. Furthermore, many Japanese words for ambition carry negative connotations such as scheming, intrigue, and social climbing.

One of the chief characteristics of paternalistic Japanese management is the *oyako* (father-son) model. As a derivative of the master-apprentice relationship, oyako functions in the modern organization, especially on the managerial level, as a vehicle by which a new employee is integrated into the department work group or the corporate family. A senior, influential employee takes charge of the trainee, subtly easing his entrance into the company and educating him regarding company norms and values.

The *senpai-kohai* (senior-junior) relationship, a corollary of *oyako*, exists at most levels in society. Plant foremen maintain close personal relations with their subordinates. Although he is unquestionably superior, the foreman is nevertheless regarded as a member of the work group, sharing their desires and destiny. Whereas in some societies constant supervision might be considered intrusive, Japanese workers expect it and recognize it as a deep personal interest in their concerns.

The quality control circle in Japan in reality is often openly controlled by management, especially when participation or interest wanes. The social importance of quality control circles is as great as their production functions. It is the company's intent not only to correct production line errors and avoid worker alienation, but also through active participation in the circles to help the worker internalize company goals. Workers are then expected to make company production goals or policies an integral part of their personal lives.

From the end of World War II until recently the personalistic and paternal model of Japanese interpersonal business relations was the norm. Certainly, there are notable exceptions to the model: Soichiro Honda (Honda) Konosuke Matsushita (Panasonic), and Genichi Kawakami (Yamaha) all rose to the ranks of zaikai without elite educational backgrounds or influential *jinmyaku.*

However, in the last ten years or so business relationships have generally become more profit oriented and less personalistic. This and other practical (in a Western sense) trends may have been caused in part by increased international trade contacts, but more importantly, current economic and technological conditions in Japan have revealed weaknesses and have forced changes on the interpersonal model. But the tradition of support by the company continues. For example, a Japanese company laid off 450 blue-collar workers in 1977–1978 because of technological transition, (from mechanical to electronics). What did this company do for their blue-collar workers?

□ Each was paid Y20,000,000 to Y40,000,000 ($100,000 to $200,000) as an indemnity.
□ The company was fully responsible for finding a new job.
□ Termination was determined as a new job was found.
□ The company supported each for vocational school.

☐ The company sponsored a "good-bye" party.
☐ All 450 got new jobs.

Slower growth has produced a surplus of mid-level managers frustrated with the lack of upward mobility under seniority-based promotion systems. This frustration has been manifested by the growing success of *heddo-hantaa* (head-hunters), executive recruitment firms. Although they were considered disreputable ten years ago, it is reported that there are now 178 licensed and unlicensed firms recruiting managers for other companies. Corporations have been attempting to protect their best young managers by offering more financial benefits—loans and bonuses—and also by beginning to seriously consider revision of the seniority-based system in favor of promotion by talent or experience.

There may also be occurring an entrepreneurial renaissance born of high-technology industries. Ken Hayashibara, President of Hayashibara Biochemical Laboratories, says:

"People of the old generation think that expansion is the main goal of a company. But to be innovative, to create new things, it helps to not grow big."

"Light, thin, short, and small" were keys to success in business between 1980 and 1984 according to Japanese executives. The younger management of high-technology electronics, chemicals, and computer firms value a "Silicon Valley"-type ambiance, emphasizing informality and creativity in the work place. And as Ken Hayashibara indicated, the inhibition of expansion is fundamental to success in creative terms.

To the extent that talented managers become frustrated and switch companies and small high-technology firms assume importance in the economy, traditional Japanese interpersonal business relations would appear to be entering a process of transformation.

With this background on Japan, you are now prepared to consider "ground rules" for negotiating with your Japanese counterpart.

4

Ground Rules for Negotiators

*T*he successful negotiation between Japanese and Western businessmen usually ends up looking very much like one between two Japanese. The visiting executive never lets on what he is really thinking, has unending patience, and is unfailingly polite. In short, he acts very Japanese.

"The Negotiating Waltz"
Time, August 1, 1983

A successful negotiation is a "win-win situation" in which both parties gain. Several intangible factors affect its outcome, such as how consistent the negotiator's acts are with the other party's values, the approach he uses, his attitude, the negotiating methods he employs, and the concern he exhibits for the other side's feelings and needs. Negotiation comprises all of these factors. The manner then in which a negotiator goes about trying to achieve his objectives may by itself meet some of the other party's needs and lead the way to agreement on the tangible issues for which the negotiation was arranged.

This chapter is about preparing for successful negotiating meetings with Japanese businessmen.

Success in negotiating with Japanese negotiators can be defined by three criteria: (1) obtaining a favorable goal, (2) reaching the solution within a reasonable time period, and (3) establishing and maintaining a positive interpersonal relationship between the negotiators. A successful negotiation requires skill, flexibility of behavior, and, as Gary Whitney suggests, the following preparatory steps:

☐ Determine the issues
☐ Know your objectives
☐ Be able to manipulate the environment
☐ Plan tactics

Determine the Issues

The first step in effective preparation, therefore, is to identify the issues one wishes to settle. In discussing the issues with one's colleagues, it is also important to develop an understanding of the Japanese negotiator's issues and psychological needs. Issues refer to goals and aspirations of the negotiation settlement. Psychological needs are important because your counterparts do not necessarily perceive the negotiation as you do, nor are the same feelings aroused during the process. It is necessary to recognize that your Japanese counterpart may be concerned with saving face.

The relevance of aspiration levels in this stage of pre-negotiation preparation is that you can never be sure of your counterpart's aspiration level. Indeed, the aspiration level is the highest goal either side attempts to achieve, and the minimum acceptable level is the least either side will accept before withdrawing from the negotiation. Therefore, you must recognize that the Japanese negotiator's aspiration level is not necessarily in line with yours.

The final step in the analysis of issues is to determine interpersonal communication expectations after the negotiation. The following are potential post-negotiation relationships:

☐ No interdependence
☐ Continued interaction with weak interdependence
☐ Vital interdependence

In the first case, your concern is to achieve the material goal, and there is little concern about offending the other party. This is almost never the case in Japanese business relationships. The second case is usually found in situations where you expect to have continued post-negotiation contact with the other party. An example of this relationship is when trust and goodwill is needed after the negotiation settlement. The third possibility, interdependence, is extremely important if the negotiating parties are closely related businesses and one depends upon the other. In other words, when closely related businesses negotiate, great care is taken to maintain a mutually productive post-negotiation relationship.

Awareness of Objectives

All negotiators agree that it is important to know what one wants to accomplish before beginning the negotiation process. Goals should be determined for each component of major issues and these goals must be outlined in order of importance.

In this regard, the Japanese and the Americans should prepare a mutually acceptable agenda early in the meetings to help determine which issues will be discussed and in what order they will be considered. An agenda acceptable to both is developed in the meeting.

The location of the negotiation is also a factor that should be considered. In Japanese-U.S. negotiations, meetings take place in Japan, the United States, and sometimes in a third country. Home country location is a factor in determining the number of negotiators on each side, entertainment, agenda, and the accommodations.

Planning

In some ways, planning for negotiations with a Japanese company is not dramatically different than planning for negotiations with an American company. Objectives will be set, strategies will be formulated, and fall-back positions will be determined. However, international business negotiations involve more than the interaction between negotiators in the formal negotiating sessions. Each negotiator is faced with factors that constrain or compel certain behaviors, techniques, and concessions. The skillful negotiator must be aware of these factors in order to anticipate both what is possible and what is impossible for the other party. Ashok Kapoor's model of negotiation classifies these factors and their effect on the negotiation process which he calls: (1) the four C's, (2) the environmental context, and (3) the broad perspective.

The Four C's—The negotiation takes place between two parties that are both drawn together and separated from each other. The negotiation takes place within this context. Kapoor identified these forces as common interests, conflicting interests, compromise, and criteria (that is, objectives for successful completion). These factors are usually set, at least in part, by the organization and are, therefore, out of the total control of the negotiator. In this sense, the negotiation takes place within boundaries set by the organization establishing primarily the issues to be negotiated.

Environmental Context—Just as the two negotiating teams operate within the context established by the firm, both the negotiating teams and the firms operate within larger contexts. The companies function under both individual and national economic pressures. There are certain cultural and social attitudes that the negotiators feel they must fulfill. Political pressure may be brought to bear upon either the negotiator or the organization. These factors will determine some of the issues to be negotiated, but primarily the techniques and strategies employed in the negotiation.

Broad Perspective—There are factors beyond the scope of organizations from both countries/cultures. These occur because of the interactions of organizations and countries on a worldwide basis. One needs to try to answer the question "What other factors may affect the outcome of this negotiation?"

Having analyzed the negotiation within its three-level context, the negotiator is now aware of the boundaries within which the negotiation has a reasonable chance for success. Strategies and techniques to be employed should be considered in relation to the total context of the negotiation to ensure success. The lesson is that strategies and techniques developed in the light of a perceived negotiation context must be flexible so they may be altered as needed when the situation changes.

Negotiation Phases

All negotiations go through the same basic phases. According to John Graham, these phases are:

- ☐ Non-task sounding
- ☐ Task-related exchange of information
- ☐ Persuasion
- ☐ Concessions

Non-Task Sounding

Negotiations begin with an attempt to get to know one's counterparts. There is an attempt to develop a rapport between the two teams, to feel out the others' personalities. The purpose is to develop a picture of the counterparts in order to be better able to anticipate strategies and reactions of the others during the negotiations.

In the United States, this is typically very short and informal. It may be as short as the introductions and exchange of pleasantries at the beginning of the first session. Graham noted that the Japanese non-task sounding tends to be both more formal and last longer than that of the United States. They are likely to include both extensive time within negotiation sessions and more relaxed meetings outside the formal sessions.

Task-Related Exchange of Information

In this stage of negotiations, the parties set the boundaries of the negotiations. They express their needs that must be fulfilled through the negotiation, various alternatives open to the parties, and their preferences among the proposed solutions. This is usually done through presentations, questions about the presentation, and proposals.

Among the Japanese, this stage comprises the primary part of the negotiation. The Japanese are trying to get complete understanding of all factors that face their opponents. According to Graham, in both actual negotiations and in controlled laboratory exercises, *"Japanese were observed to spend much more time trying to understand the situation and associated details of another position."*

Graham also noted frustration on the American side during this stage. The Americans tended to provide information directly, using clear and precise statements. By American standards, the Japanese response seemed too evasive but the Japanese negotiators were trying to fulfill their cultural standards of *tatemae* and *honne*. *Tatemae* can be translated as a principle or policy that is the "official" stance on an issue. *Honne* is "true mind" or the real intention. If negative feelings are present and these may offend, the cultural requirement of a Japanese is to withhold the honne to maintain harmony. The result to the Japanese is the maintenance of relationships in which agreement can be made; to the Americans, the result is a rather confusing statement that is perceived as evasive or perhaps dishonest.

The problems that begin to surface here are a fundamental difference in perception of the purpose of the negotiation. Americans try to satisfactorily resolve the *issue;* Japanese try to establish a satisfactory *relationship* with the other party, assuming that once the relationship is established, the issue will basically resolve itself.

Concessions

At this point in the negotiation, the parties are usually separated by different perceived solutions. Neither party is satisfied and the job becomes one of convincing the other side to modify its positions.

In this stage, once again we see the difference in approach by Japanese and American negotiators. To the Japanese, if a relationship of trust has been achieved with the opposition, the differences can be worked out. It may not be easy, but a final agreement is nearly assured.

At some point in all successful negotiations, the positions of the parties are modified and an agreement is reached. The concessions made by the parties may be made at the end of negotiations or at various points within the negotiations.

To Americans, concessions are made over the entire course of the negotiation. They tend to be made sequentially, that is, with subsequent agreements dependent on previous ones. The final agreement becomes a summary of all the previous agreements.

To the Japanese, concessions and agreements usually come at the end of negotiations. They come from agreeing to individual items that result in a total agreement. This seems abrupt from an American negotiating perspective.

The extreme cultural dissimilarity in what each culture perceives as "acceptable" behavior creates much frustration when the Japanese and Americans attempt to negotiate. Americans are particularly troubled by the perceived ambiguity of the Japanese as well as any delayed responses. In fact, Americans often try to fill in the silence with conversation. The negotiation then becomes a monologue rather than a constructive dialogue. The Japanese are made uncomfortable by the Americans' need to persuade and to hurry the negotiations.

Aside from extreme differences in the perception of how to conduct the negotiation, the understanding of status orientation and the significance of situational constraints are also dissimilar and lead to the termination of cross-cultural negotiations. According to Graham, this aspect of Japanese/American business negotiations is most relevant vis-a-vis its implications for management of business relations between the two cultures.

In Japan, interpersonal relationships are vertically structured. In other words, in business relationships, a class distinction is evident based on factors, including: age, sex, education, position in a firm. Therefore, the Japanese must be aware of status of each negotiator in order to know how to act in a business interaction. While the Japanese are ill at ease if a class distinction between two individuals is uncertain, Americans hold very little relevance to this aspect of a relationship, nor do they adjust behavior accordingly. In fact, quite the opposite is true—Americans are likely to establish interpersonal status equality.

These differences in status orientation manifested themselves in Graham's simulated business negotiation. Results from his experiment indicate that when Americans negotiate, honest information from opponents was important in obtaining one's goals. For this same experiment, using Japanese negotiators, results were the converse; i.e., credible bargaining tactics were not effective in the achievement of one's profit goals. Further, in terms of the American negotiations, the role of the negotiator (buyer versus seller) was not relevant to negotiation performance. In other words, on the whole, buyers and sellers were equally matched in performance level. Yet, in the Japanese negotiations, the most important factor in explaining the success of the negotiator was his *role*. That is, buyers achieved a higher profit in the negotiation than sellers. Therefore, *while Americans expect to affect negotiation outcomes as a result of the bargaining, the Japanese negotiation outcome is more predetermined by status relations.*

An additional aspect of the Japanese vertical structure of relationships that is important to understand is that while the Japanese buyer has the freedom to choose a deal he wants, he is always responsible for considering the needs of the seller. The cultural norm, *amae* (indulgent dependency), assures that one's business opponent can be trusted.

Finally, the most illustrative description of the way in which relationships are structured in Japan is to use a comparison. In Japan, bargaining is a process that is similar to the way a father and son interact. The buyer is the one in the controlling position—i.e., the father—and the seller must be very cautious in his approach to the buyer—i.e., just as a son must be careful, respectful, etc. in his approach to his father if he expects to obtain what he wants.

Considering the apparent differences in the structural relationships between the Japanese and American cultures, how does this affect negotiations? The Japanese seller and American buyer generally get along well, whereas the American seller will not be as accepted by the Japanese buyer. Further, Graham contends that major trade difficulties between these two cultures stem from the concept of interpersonal relationship status and his experiments are supportive of his contentions.

In both the laboratory experiments and in actual cross-cultural negotiations, the Japanese did adapt themselves to the American style of conducting business. American negotiators did not make analogous adjustments. Why is there a difference? The reasoning lies in what anthropologists refer to as power relations—i.e., which party adapts and which party adopts in inter-cultural relations reflects one's power status in the relationship. Interestingly, the results would have been quite different had the interaction taken place in Japan where the power structure is definitively hierarchical. In other words, had an American buyer gone to Japan expecting the Japanese seller to treat him honorably and with equal respect, the Japanese would be perturbed by this rather brash behavior of the American. The negotiation would be likely to end quite abruptly and without explanation on the part of the Japanese seller. In fact, this business outcome commonly occurs. Unfortunately, the Japanese system is rarely learned by Americans because the door is either closed or only open a little and American negotiators get discouraged in trying to enter.

Persuasion

To American negotiators, the key to successful negotiating is the ability to persuade their counterparts to change. Most books and articles center on various techniques to strengthen one's ability to persuade or to resist the persuasions of the other. However, the Japanese operate within a different persuading context, and American persuasion techniques must be altered to be effective with the Japanese.

An influence style is the technique an individual uses to convince another person to act in a desired way. Each person uses different influence styles depending on who the other person is and a series of factors surrounding the desired action. However, negotiators find it easy to influence others in a certain way and; therefore, use these styles.

Four styles of persuasion identified by Situation Management Systems, Inc. in their negotiation research are:

Factual—A person operating in the factual influence style believes that a presentation of facts will convince someone. Hence, there is an emphasis on documentation and details.

Intuitive—A person operating in the intuitive influence style tries to influence by emphasizing the benefits of a solution. The emphasis is on an imaginative approach to new possibilities.

Normative—The normative style is to influence by appeal to a common system of beliefs. The emphasis is on reaching a "fair" solution. Behavior tends to be based on emotions, using such tactics as threats, authority, rewards, and incentives to reach a compromise.

Analytical—A person using this style tries to influence another by showing causal relationships. The emphasis is on establishing the relationship between parts and then synthesizing them into a whole.

In attempting to convince someone, influence styles should be integrated and used simultaneously. An intuitive person has a difficult time convincing a factual person using the intuitive influence style. The intuitive person will eventually use some of the characteristics of the factual influence style in order to succeed.

Successful persuasion involves two factors: (1) the influence style profile of the persuader (see questionnaire in Appendix A), and (2) the persuader must evaluate the influence style of person to be persuaded. It is recommended that Appendix A be completed and studied prior to one's next negotiations with Japanese businessmen. The scores should be entered on the profile and the guidelines studied.

Persuasion in Japan

According to Graham, Americans perceive the negotiation as an opportunity to forge agreements out of debate and confrontation. The attempts at persuasion take place, for the most part, at the negotiation table. On the other hand, Japanese perceive the negotiation almost as the ritualistic enactment of a predetermined agreement. They look with horror on the confrontation that Americans expect at the table. Rather, the Japanese prefer to attempt persuasion behind the scenes, where neither side is in danger of losing face.

Japan is basically a vertical society, and positions within the society are clearly defined. Graham noted that in negotiations among Japanese, discussion might take place, but the results seemed to favor the person with the highest status. It appears that it is social position, not ideas, that persuades. In Graham's study, American-Japanese negotiations ran into difficulty most often when the Japanese perceived himself to be of greater status. At this point, the two parties try to persuade in different arenas: the American with ideas and the Japanese with position. Both sides end up frustrated.

Graham also noted the relationship between persuasion, emotion, and culture. Americans negotiating with Americans tend to achieve higher profits by making the other party feel uncomfortable. Japanese tend to do the opposite. They achieved greater profits by making the other party feel comfortable. Perhaps this is the reason that Eliot McGinnies (as related by Howard F. Van Zandt) noted that Japanese university students were more responsive to persuasive arguments that were two-sided, as opposed to one-sided arguments. Van Zandt also noticed that Japanese are more likely to be persuaded by a written presentation than an oral presentation: "The Japanese feel that when a man is willing to put his case in print, where all may challenge what he has said, it is likely that he will be accurate so as not to lose face."

Use of Logic

Regardless of the influence style used, the persuader uses some form of logic in order to convince the other. The persuader does everything possible to make the presentation as reasonable as possible or, in other words, to make it logical. The problem is that logical thought processes differ between Americans and Japanese. It is important to note that many Japanese have developed the ability to use and understand Western logic through extensive contact or perhaps a period of living in the West. However, their most comfortable way of thinking remains Japanese.

Masao Kunihiro says the difference is that Japanese statements fall into one of two categories. In the first, items are presented in a highly anecdotal or episodic way. The conclusions are seldom articulated. The typical American response is "So what?" The second method is to reason deductively by presenting data. The typical American response is "That may be, but we need more specifics." American presentations start with data and move to generalities and conclusions. This evokes a similar response of incompleteness from the Japanese. The result is that a presentation that appears perfectly logical to one group seems nearly incomprehensible to the other.

Glen Fisher says the difference between Japanese and American logic is that the Japanese language "lends its user to decide *what* something is rather than *why* it should be that way." The descriptions seem endless to Americans, and the cause-effect relationships seem inane to Japanese. Fisher also suggests that the Japanese have a tendency to distrust the attempt to use language to develop support of a given point of view.

In addition to differences in the logic process, words possess different connotations in the different culture. For instance, Masao relates the following statement by President Nixon in China: "China and the United States share many parallel interests and can do much together." Both cultures understand that the word "parallel" means "with like direction or tendency." However, Americans use the word parallel to emphasize similarity. To Japanese, parallel emphasizes the impossibility of two lines converging, implying a position of opposition or confrontation.

Strategy

John Ilich in *The Art and Skill of Successful Negotiation* says the negotiator should attempt to take the offensive as early in the negotiation process as possible:

> "He should take the offensive whenever he feels he can do so without his opponent being consciously aware of the change. . . . Once you have the offensive, it is seldom wise to pause or to play a defensive or conservative hand. The defensive player recovers a fumble and runs for a touchdown; he has turned his thoughts to offensive tactics the moment he grabbed the ball and glanced down the field toward his opponent's goal . . ."

While this "football" approach to negotiation may seem valid for Americans negotiating with other Americans, how would this approach work with Japanese negotiators who seek mutual interests in a negotiation, who dislike vying for power, are reluctant to enter into arguments, and perhaps have little understanding of the concepts of "offensive" and "defensive"? What kind of effect would "good guy, bad guy," "hand on the doorknob" or other such strategies have? One would expect to find this adversarial outlook more in an unhealthy "win-lose approach" to negotiation as opposed to a "win-win" situation where both parties gain. Unfortunately, this game approach to negotiations is frequently used by American negotiators.

Strategy is an overall approach that considers the important objectives of the negotiations. Tactics, on the other hand, are the maneuvers and actions that implement a strategy and permit the accomplishment of an objective. Negotiation tactics may be planned in advance, or they may be chosen as a given situation arises. Although the focus in this material is *not* on tactics but rather on developing skillful win-win negotiations, a brief review of tactics commonly used by American negotiators may be helpful.

Agendas are used to establish a certain control in the negotiation. It should cover in general terms the areas you seek to discuss.

Questions can be used in a number of ways to seek information, to avoid answering a question, to stall for time, or create controversy. The side that asks the questions controls the process of negotiation and generally accomplishes more in bargaining situations. There are four kinds of questions.

- ☐ Direct questions—Addressed to a specific person, they force the other party to make some kind of response.
- ☐ Leading questions—Device that forces the other side to take a position on a specific area.
- ☐ Provocative questions—Tend to evoke an emotional and often hostile response in the other party.
- ☐ Yes or No questions—Attempt to force the other side into a decision posture.

Concessions are used to determine what a seller really wants, the extent of his desire, and what he is willing to give up to achieve that desire. The idea behind the concession is for the buyer to give up as little as possible in order to gain a concession of greater value.

According to Gavin Kennedy in *Managing Negotiations:* "Negotiation is about removing the padding on the opposition's proposals." He suggests that the following tactics are used by American negotiators routinely:

- ☐ *Trial Balloons*—The tactics of introducing a subject, making a proposal or stating a demand with the words "What if. . . ." While the proposal usually has little chance of being accepted, the idea is to test the reactions of the other side and their strength of conviction. Trial balloons help a negotiator to avoid the need to take a stand that could commit him to a point of view too early in the negotiation. Too many "trial balloons" with Japanese negotiators result in feelings of distrust.

☐ *Nibbling*—A commonly used technique of constantly scrambling for small concessions on a given subject. If it becomes clear early in the negotiation that it will be difficult to get the whole package, this tactic makes sense. The theory behind it is that it may be possible to negotiate small items one at a time and so end up with the bulk of the whole. It is a technique that builds a climate of confidence and a track record on a gradual basis. Japanese negotiators often use this tactic.

☐ *Good Guy-Bad Guy*—A technique that requires at least two team members. One person behaves aggressively while his team member keeps a quieter profile. One problem with this tactic with Japanese negotiators is that it is a disruptive force that triggers hostility when cooperation and support are more important.

☐ *Greater Rewards (Sell Cheap, Get Famous)*—The "carrot principle," a very common tactic for getting a compromise. Usually, it is most effective toward the end of a negotiation, because it is based on the hope that the possibility of greater rewards (i.e., future orders, etc. . .) will motivate the negotiator to make concessions. This does not work with the Japanese, as they conceptualize relationships as long term anyway.

☐ *Noah's Ark*—When a buyer says, "You will have to do much better than the price you suggested. I have proposals from your competitors that offer me much better terms," it is almost always a bluff. If he has better terms, he has no need to negotiate with you.

This list of tactics could go on: deadlocks, walk-outs, undermining, changing the subject, going for a quick close, etc. A detailed examination of all tactics would lead one to conclude that the frequent use of any of these is a bad idea when negotiating with the Japanese. Before using tactics, one should carefully consider the other team's potential reaction. While the Japanese might appear to be "soggy noodles" to U.S. negotiators, they may in fact be considering a proposal or indicating difficulty in accepting it. Americans tend to overreact to these periods of silence by granting concessions, by responding with threats and warnings, or by pushing too far even when the other side may be clearly signaling "no." A negotiation failure is not far off when this is the case.

Conclusion

It is impossible to stop being an American at the negotiating table. It is impossible and undesirable to try to "become Japanese." When preparing strategies, avoid presentations that rely heavily on American persuasion techniques, and if negotiations falter, consider how persuasion techniques might be altered to be more effective with Japanese negotiators.

Learn to manage the negotiations. Successful negotiations with the Japanese emphasize the importance of prenegotiation planning, appropriate interpersonal behavior, understanding how to present the proposal, and the correct style of approach.

5

"Secrets" of Successful Negotiators

Introduction

"*F*oreigners seldom understand what any controversy is about; they do not know what is being left unsaid because it is unnecessary to say it, or what is behind the dazzling smiles, the hearty embraces, the damp kisses on stubby cheeks, the clasped hands, the compliments, the declarations of eternal friendship."

Luigi Barzini

"The Americans will tell you that contracts were not lived up to. What do the Americans mean? They thought they had a meeting of minds once the clauses of the contract were verbalized. They failed to realize that these declarations of intent were only the beginning—not the end—of the negotiations. They went ahead with their investments without having spent the time nailing down the fine points. . . . Thus they lost out."

Douglas F. Lamont

Most literature on business negotiations contains statements of advice, admonition, reflections such as the preceding quotations. Books or seminars on negotiations can be categorized in two general areas:

☐ "Stories of what I did or heard." These stories are interesting and often entertaining, but are difficult to learn from or serve as a guide for future negotiators.
☐ Highly theoretical models of negotiating that may be of use to academics but are of little help to people who negotiate.

There is little information on what actually happens during a negotiation and what are the differences, if any, between effective or successful negotiators and negotiators who are not effective. The material in this chapter discusses some of the skills and behavioral characteristics that are necessary for American negotiators to display when negotiating in Japan. These skills are the "secrets" of successful negotiators and they can be learned.

The Business Relationship

The importance of establishing the appropriate emotional basis for conducting negotiations is vital to successfully doing business in Japan. For example, an employee of a Japanese trading company assigned to work in Latin America was once told, "Don't engage in business for one year—just get acquainted with people." So, he learned to socialize and to speak Spanish. His amiability was extremely beneficial when he did begin negotiations. This illustration can apply to Americans doing business in Japan. In fact, it is imperative if one is to be accepted and successful.

In Japan, socializing is a vital component of doing business. Participation in activities such as golf, visiting cabarets or bars, and invitations to watch sumo matches are an integral part of establishing favorable business relationships. Business lunches are also vital to doing business in Japan. "After five" entertainment is even more important.

Gift-giving is another well-known factor in maintaining or establishing an important business rapport. Gifts are sometimes very expensive, although most gifts range from $25 to $50. All are carefully selected and presented.

Once a proposed negotiation is of interest to a Japanese company, meetings would be arranged. The Japanese are very meticulous, and therefore you must provide visual aids (i.e., graphs, diagrams, sketches, slides) during a presentation. This is useful supplementary material for the verbal message. The Japanese use the meetings as a time to carefully analyze their counterparts. Final decisions about the negotiation are then made as a group and no decision is left to just one individual.

The Japanese value sincerity. It is common during negotiations for the Japanese to mention a high-quality, competitive producer. Doing so indicates that one's company is outwardly honest and acknowledges other companies of high integrity. Further, the Japanese usually put their proposals and market plan in writing. This procedure shows that the company believes enough in its product to allow it to be challenged. The American negotiator is wise to follow similar procedures. This also reduces misunderstandings.

Communication Skills

Communication involves the exchange of a message from a sender to a receiver. The process is complicated, but basically a message is encoded with meaning, communicated through voice, gestures, postures, facial expressions, or eye movements and decoded by the receiver. The decoding depends on external factors, such as the environment or social setting, and a myriad of internal factors pertaining to the receiver, such as background, experiences, emotions, education, expectations, etc. With all these internal "voices" working on the receiver, some messages get lost in misunderstandings. When "culture" is added to the mix of influences, the people communicating are even further separated in terms of experiences and expectations, and must "shout" over a wider chasm to understand each other. Americans belong to a very "low context" culture in which a great proportion of information is "spelled out," we want to be told clearly and specifically what is on the other person's mind. Americans attach great importance to what is "said" and often literally believe what they "hear" and take people at their "word." Many is the time in a business or social misunderstanding, a confused party will protest "but he said . . ." defending one's interpretation of the situation.

The Japanese, on the other hand belong to a relatively "high context" culture; they consider the spoken word to be only one part of the total picture and the message to convey several levels of meaning. One level, the true meaning, may be quite contradictory to the literal meaning of the words. The language is subtle, an emphasis on a syllable or vowel can change the entire meaning of the word. A great deal in Japanese culture is "understood" without the use of words, partly because of the cultural homogeneity. A Japanese, therefore, when establishing a personal relationship with an American may look for cues of "meaning" underneath the spoken words and an American may be literally "saying what he means" and expecting the same in return. For example, a common situation that occurs when Americans work for Japanese is a sense of frustration at not being told precisely "what to do" and "what they want." The messages may have already been given countless times in a variety of ways and the Japanese employer cannot understand the confusion surrounding duties, deadlines, etc.

The emphasis in the United States is on making oneself understood; the emphasis in Japan is on understanding "where the other person is coming from."

Once the American business negotiator is aware of potential problems in cross-cultural communication, a strategy is needed to deal with anticipated conflicts. First, says Graham, negotiators must go to Japan ready to adjust their behavior to fit the Japanese style. He outlines four causes of communication ineffectiveness; which are presented in order of increasing complexity:

Language/language behaviors—While it is an obvious advantage to be able to speak the Japanese language, this is rarely the case; considering the small amount of time that executives are in Japan, language fluency is expensive training. However, the inability to speak Japanese means that one is less apt to pick up nonverbal cues and more delayed time occurs in the translation process.

Nonverbal behavior—Most Americans working with Japanese do not learn the language and therefore a basic understanding of nonverbal cues is even more important. In Japan, nonverbal signals are very unlike American signals. For example, in Japan, there is markedly less eye contact and more silence. These are very normal behaviors for the Japanese. American negotiators must be tuned in to these cues so as not to misread them.

Values—One major potential difficulty in negotiations is the Japanese value system referred to earlier of *honne* ("true mind"), *tatemae* ("public statement"), and *amae* ("the need to be needed, wanted, and accepted"). The Japanese are very polite and prefer not to show their feelings so as not to risk disrupting harmony. Because the Japanese rarely express negative thoughts or answer "no," it is vital that Americans be able to test them for their feelings on a topic. An effective strategy is for negotiators to ask the Japanese more questions. This is the best way to understanding their viewpoint and positions.

Decision processes—Earlier, it was noted that the Japanese decision-making process is quite different from the Americans'. For example, in Japan, much more time is required to develop a harmonious interpersonal relationship. In other words, Americans must foresee the procedural differences, have patience, and time their strategies to suit the Japanese decision-making style in negotiating.

The importance of status in establishing the Japanese interpersonal decision-making process merits reiteration. Americans must be very conscious of the vertical structure of class distinction and be very careful to respect this system of negotiation, if a successful outcome is to be achieved.

Pierre Casse in *Training for the Cross-Cultural Mind* defines what he terms as the "Five International Negotiating Skills":

☐ To be able to practice empathy and to see the world as other people see it. To understand others' behavior from their perspective.

□ To be able to demonstrate the advantages of one's proposals so that the counterparts in the negotiation will be willing to change.

□ To be able to manage stress and cope with ambiguous situations as well as unpredictable demands.

□ To be able to express one's own ideas in such a way that
the people one negotiates with will objectively and fully
understand what one has in mind.

□ To be sensitive to the cultural background of others and
adjust the suggestions one wants to make to the existing
constraints and limitations.

The skills are general but can serve as a guideline to determine your preparedness to negotiate effectively in Japan.

Listening Skills

Listening is indeed an overlooked, underrated skill. High-sta-
tus Americans such as middle and top managers often suffer
from an "I told you so" syndrome. They may have only a general
idea about what is happening during a meeting and will only
partially listen to opinions and comments, often finishing others' sentences with their own choice words. Americans tend to
interrupt, which is considered rude in Japan. Especially in dealings with foreigners who do not have a mastery of the English
language, it is tempting to "help along" by inserting words and
phrases when pauses are seen as a searching for the correct expression.

The Japanese have a great deal less compulsion to formulate
instant judgments and answers. They will often pause a moment
before commenting or answering, considering carefully what
has been said. In a negotiating session, one person may even
have the sole task of listening to the other side. Think of the
enormous advantage that offers in terms of perceiving the
"whole picture" of a session. Japanese are told to "look at the
forest, don't look only at the trees." Americans, when they interrupt, are seen as unduly impatient, aggressive, and even lacking
respect for the person who has spoken. As an exercise in listening skills, it might be a good idea to feed back ideas to a speaker

in your own words, such as "What I hear you saying is . . . ," and test your own perceptions of what was said. Change roles and repeat the process. During the session carefully consider what is said and write down any points of misunderstanding that might especially be due to cultural differences, mistranslations, or mis-interpretations of key concepts. Do not hesitate to clarify these points later, explaining that you understand the possibility that the cultural context influences ways of doing business and you want to ensure that this does not interfere with a harmonious business relationship.

Americans also tend to perceive the person most fluent in your own language to be the "leader" or the most intelligent member of the other team. A large portion of time or energy is then directed toward that person, trying to convince or impress him. This could be a serious error across the negotiating table since many top level Japanese executives do not have an excel-lent command of English and generally no one person is present at a session who has the sole authority to make a decision.

Asking Questions

Americans are rewarded from an early age for being inquisi-tive and asking direct and pointed questions. In business meet-ings, those who ask questions are perceived as bright and knowledgeable. Japanese are generally more reserved in public and are uncomfortable with a confrontative, debative style of questioning. They use questions to guide rather than confront in business meetings. Due to the cultural value of "saving face," they may not wish to put someone on the spot or embarrass him. The question-and-answer periods are more formalized and reserved until the end of a presentation or session. Do not inter-pret the lack of questions as a lack of understanding. This could lead to some embarrassing situations such as drawing up a con-tract based on what was thought or assumed to be a mutual agreement. The nod of a head or the reply *"hai"* (yes) does not necessarily agree with the English equivalent of "yes." Clearly express your desire for opinions without being pushy in order to avoid future misunderstanding. It may also be wise to break up the meeting into smaller groups with more time set aside for question-and-answer periods.

If a Japanese interprets a question as being too direct or specific, he may pause before answering, considering how to respond or avoid a direct answer. He may even refrain from answering the question altogether. If this happens, do not assume that you were not understood and repeat the question. Also do not assume you are being ignored or evaded. Wait to rephrase the question at a later time or consider dropping the question altogether until you can analyze the situation and determine why the question was an uncomfortable one.

Speaking Styles

Public speaking ability is a highly rewarded skill in American culture. To "speak up" is to be assertive and courageous. Eloquence in persuasion is taught in seminars throughout the country. In contrast, Japanese place much more importance on the written language. Japanese speakers tend to express themselves in a softer, less emotional manner, relying more on formalized patterns of speech. This may seem insincere or unassertive to Americans. On the other hand, Japanese view Americans as talking too much in general and specifically talking too much about their own accomplishments and abilities. This is seen as self-promotion and does not impress the Japanese. The most effective method of speaking is a step-by-step explanation of every point, especially when introducing new products or ideas. Negotiators should keep their "cool" even in the most frustrating of circumstances.

Silence

Americans associate silence in a negative context: anxiety, hostility, awkwardness, or shyness. Silences are not empty spaces to be filled with words in Japan, but moments to be shared. A silence can mean respect for the person who has spoken, consideration of an important point, or disagreement with what has been suggested. During a meeting there are often long periods of silence that are broken by Americans who often feel anxious. Americans will deal with silence by repeating or elaborating upon a point or making concessions unnecessarily. The best way to handle an awkward period of silence is to accept the silence and use the time to review points that were made in the discussion. If the silence becomes unbearable, it may be wise to request a short break.

Directness and Indirectness

Americans value "laying cards on the table," being direct and to the "point." Americans are also viewed by the Japanese as tending to be preoccupied with being rational and logical. On the other hand, Americans tend to see Japanese as slow, subjective, and practical. Directness in Japanese culture is interpreted as insensitive to others' feelings. Particularly among equals in social status, directness is seen as "commanding" behavior such as a general commands troops. Hours of discussion may take place across a negotiating table before there is an inkling of an idea what the Japanese team is driving at. In the meantime many damaging assumptions may be made as to intent and acted upon in a hasty and impulsive manner by the American team. Since it is difficult to avoid directness for anyone raised in an American cultural context, the best technique would be awareness and sensitivity toward what might be interpreted by Japanese as being overly direct behavior. Questions such as "What do you think about the proposal?" can put someone on the spot since any Japanese would feel uncomfortable making a decision or voicing an opinion for the entire team.

Nonverbal Communication

People are often unaware of how they are constantly communicating through their "body language" including gestures, posture, facial expressions, and eye movements. There are many nonverbal signals unique to certain cultures and many signals that are interpreted differently in different cultural settings. Americans are generally very casual and informal in their attitudes. This is exhibited especially when attempting to address foreign business colleagues on a first name basis. Americans often slouch or lean back in chairs and cross their legs when feeling comfortable or as a reaction to a stressful situation. These positions may be interpreted as "not caring" or "not being serious about the matter at hand." Japanese are very sensitive to "body language" and are able to pick up more information from Westerners when there is a spoken language barrier.

Skills of Successful Negotiators

The following is a summary* of a research project that analyzed *actual* negotiations. The researchers' methods allowed them to differentiate between skilled negotiators and average negotiators by using behavior analysis techniques as they ob-

---

* *Behavior of Successful Negotiators,* Huthwaite Research Group Report, 1976, 1982.

served the negotiations and recorded the discussion. They identified "successful" negotiators as those who—

☐ Were rated as effective by both sides.
☐ Had a "track-record" of significant success.
☐ Had a low incidence of "implementation" failures.

A total of 48 negotiators were studied who met all of these three
success criteria. They included:

Union representatives (17)
Management representatives (12)
Contract negotiators (10)
Others (9)

The 48 successful negotiators were studied over a total of 102
separate negotiating sessions. In the following description, the
successful negotiators are called the "skilled" group. In comparison, the negotiators who either failed to meet the criteria or
about whom no criterion data were available, were called the
"average" group.

During the Planning Process

Negotiation training emphasizes the importance of planning.

☐ *Planning time*—No significant difference was found between the total planning time that skilled and average negotiators claimed they spent prior to actual negotiation.

☐ *Exploration of Options*—The skilled negotiator considers
a wider range of outcomes or options for action, than the
average negotiator.
Skilled negotiator—5.1 outcomes or options/issue
Average negotiator—2.6 outcomes or options/issue

☐ *Common Ground*—The research showed that the skilled
negotiators gave over three times as much attention to
common ground areas as did average negotiators.

Skilled negotiators—38% of comments about areas of anticipated agreement or common ground
Average negotiators—11% of comments about areas of anticipated agreement or common ground

☐ *Long-Term or Short-Term?*—With the average negotiator, approximately one comment in 25 met the criteria of a long-term consideration, namely a comment that involved any factor extending beyond the immediate implementation of the issue under negotiation. The skilled negotiator, while showing twice as many long-term comments, still only averages 8.5% of his total recorded planning comment.

☐ *Setting Limits*—The researchers asked negotiators about their objectives and recorded whether their replies referred to single-point objectives (e.g., "We aim to settle at 83") or to a defined range (e.g., "We hope to get 85 but we would settle for a minimum of 77"). Skilled negotiators were significantly more likely to set upper and lower limits—to plan in terms of range. Average negotiators, in contrast, were more likely to plan their objectives around a fixed point.

☐ *Sequence and Issue Planning*—The term "planning" frequently refers to a process of sequencing—putting a number of events, points, or potential occurrences into a time sequence. Critical path analysis and other forms of network planning are examples.

Typical sequence plan used by average negotiators

A   then   B   then   C   then   D
in which issues are linked.

Typical issue plan used by skilled negotiators

A

B

D

C

in which issues are independent and not linked
by sequence

	Number of Mentions Implying Sequence in Planning
Skilled negotiators	2.1 per session
Average negotiators	4.9 per session

The clear advantage of issue planning over sequence planning is flexibility.

Face-To-Face Behavior

Skilled negotiators show marked differences in their face-to-face behavior, compared with average negotiators. They use certain types of behavior significantly more frequently while other types they tend to avoid.

☐ *Irritators*—Certain words and phrases that are commonly used during negotiation have negligible value in persuading the other party, but do cause irritation. Probably the most frequent example of these is the term "generous offer" used by a negotiator to describe his own proposal.

	Use of Irritators Per Hour Face-To-Face Speaking Time
Skilled negotiators	2.3
Average negotiators	10.8

☐ *Counter Proposals*—During negotiation, one party frequently puts forward a proposal and the other party immediately responds with a counter-proposal. Researchers found that skilled negotiators made immediate counter-proposals much less frequently than average negotiators.

	Frequency of Counter-Proposals Per Hour of Face-to-Face Speaking Time
Skilled negotiators	1.7
Average negotiators	3.1

☐ *Argument Dilution*—This way of thinking predisposes us to believe that there is some special merit in quantity. Having five reasons for doing something is considered more persuasive than having only one reason. We feel that the more we can put on our scale, the more likely we are to tip the balance of an argument in our favor.

	Average Number of Reasons Given By Negotiator to Back Each Argument/Case S/he Advanced
Skilled negotiator	1.8
Average negotiator	3.0

The researchers found that the opposite was true. The skilled negotiator used less reasons to back up each of his/her arguments.

☐ *Reviewing the Negotiation*—The researchers asked negotiators how likely they were to spend time reviewing the negotiation afterwards. Over two-thirds of the skilled negotiators claimed that they always set aside some time after a negotiation to review it and consider what they had learned. Just under half of average negotiators, in contrast, made the same claim.

This research is the best available that clearly indicates the *behavior* of skilled negotiators. These are the behaviors to imitate or avoid.

Conclusion

To negotiate effectively in Japan, the skills just identified are required for the following reasons:

☐ There may be a cultural conditioning with regard to the way negotiators view the nature of the negotiation process itself. American negotiators are often frustrated because their counterparts do not enter in the expected give-and-take, which they typically experience in domestic or labor-management negotiations in the United States.

☐ For the Japanese, to openly disagree is not a pleasant experience and whenever there is a conflict in a negotiation situation, very often a go-between or a third person is used to assist in the negotiation process.

☐ American negotiators usually begin a negotiating session by trusting the persons until proven otherwise. However for the Japanese, they would be more inclined to mistrust until faith and trust is proven by their counterparts.

☐ American negotiators view the process as a problem-solving exercise whereby a number of fall back positions are carefully discussed prior to a session. However, the Japanese do not view it as a problem-solving exercise, and their first position is often the only position they have discussed and the one they wish to present and have accepted.

☐ The role of protocol in negotiations is very important in Japan.

6

Never Take "Yes" for an Answer

Introduction

*P*rofessor Chie Nakane of Tokyo University expressed the opinion that the expression of "no" is virtually never used by Japanese outside of completely reciprocal relationships, and from a superior to an inferior. Hence, in a business relationship, it is rare to hear "no" as it is used in the West.

But western negotiators must learn to recognize a "no" answer, as it is not enough to assume that agreement has been reached. Many times the impression of agreement is given in conformity with the Asian custom of telling others what they want to hear, rather than what one's real answer might be.

This could lead to problems for the uninitiated businessman but there are ways to avoid such a situation.

Techniques of understanding a Japanese "no" when one has just heard an English "yes" have been explained in an unpublished thesis entitled, "Japanese Patterns of Declining Requests," by Keiko Ueda. In negotiations, a vague response may indicate that the individual is having a hard time making up his mind or that he has already decided in the negative. By being vague, the party spares his listener embarrassment; the soft quality of such a rejection cushions its impact. Also, vague or ambiguous uses of "yes" can give the speaker time to make up his mind, hide his confusion, or bring about the right "environment" in which to gauge the reaction of the listener.

Another technique used by the Japanese is silence. Rejection, reflection, and indecision all can exist in the silence of Japanese negotiators. What is critical for the Westerner to understand is that this silence is not used confrontationally or to create tension. It is advisable to "answer" silence with silence and take advantage of the break to reflect on what has been discussed up to that point.

Asking a counter question is another way of saying "no" in Japanese. If the Japanese negotiator is not prepared to answer the question or if the answer will be negative, the question may be turned around and readdressed to the questioner. Ueda also states that a conditional response can be used, for example, when one does not want to accept the request or demand, but when he himself feels he's in a delicate situation. The speaker may say, "yes, I will do everything in my power to comply, but if I cannot complete my task, I hope you will understand." This translates to a "yes, but" situation and generally means "no."

And finally, there is the apology approach. The Japanese are adept at making light of themselves only to make a lot of fuss

over the listener. This lays the groundwork for the speaker to assume an implicitly inferior position. His apology will reflect the
impossibility of meeting his superiors' request due to his own
inferior ability. Therefore, no explanation is required, and the re-
questor won't feel offended by the word of apology. All in all, a
very neat system.

Idiomatic Expressions — What Do They Mean?

American businessmen use idiomatic expressions routinely in
their business transactions. When speaking with persons of similar lifestyles and experiences, idiomatic expressions are easily
understood. But when an American businessman is speaking
with an American businesswoman who is not interested in or
conversant with the vocabulary of sports or military, the use of
the word "score" might result in a miscommunication. Betty Le-
han Harragan in *Games Mother Never Taught You* gives this example:

> "In the glossary of business jargon, one word is more
> important for women to recognize than all others. It
> serves as a conjunctive which joins the military mental-
> ity, organized sports, and big business. . . . The word is
> 'scoring.'
>
> *To Score:* To win a victory; to make a profitable deal;
> to accomplish a desirable act in the face of
> competition; to pile up points in your favor.
> To have sexual intercourse with a female
> peer one has aggressively pursued just for
> that purpose. . . .
>
> The same versatile word is used frequently in the female
> culture, but its associations are drastically different. It
> can mean anything from making superficial cuts in
> meat before cooking, to totaling up points in bridge or
> scrabble, to the orchestration for a musical composi-
> tion, to an indefinitely large number, as in "Scores of
> people attended."

Even among Americans, terms have different connotations.

When idiomatic expressions are used by American negotiators with Japanese negotiators, misunderstandings often result. To determine the extent that such expressions were not understood by Japanese businessmen a list of 400 business-related idioms from the *Dictionary of American Idioms* was distributed to Japanese businessmen. The results showed that over 50% of the expressions were not understood by the Japanese. The following is a list of many of these expressions, listed by topic:

Time-related idiomatic expressions—

Against time . . . against the clock
Ahead of time
At a snail's pace
At present
Better late than never
Bide one's time
Call it a day
Early bird catches the worm
Have a time
In no time
In the long run
In the nick of time
In the short run
In time
Less than no time
Let grass grow under one's feet
Make a day of it
On schedule
On the dot
On the spur of the moment
On time
Pass the time of day
Put it on the back burner
Right away
Take one's time
Time is money
Time is ripe
Time out
While away
Zero hour

Games/sports-related idiomatic expressions—

Across the board
Ahead of the game
At (this) stage of the game
Break even
Carry the ball
Game at which two can play
Get the ball rolling
Get to first base
Keep the ball rolling
Lay one's cards on the table
Long shot
Name of the game
Play the game
Running start
Set the pace
Skate on thin ice

Have two strikes against you	Ten-to-one
Hit the bull's eye	Time out
Jump the gun	Within bounds
	You bet

Military-related idiomatic expressions—

All systems go	In the line of duty
Ally	Join forces
At stake	Line of fire
Back out	Long shot
Draw fire	Lose ground
Gain ground	Quick on the trigger
Head off	Take charge
Hold the line	Under fire
	Zero hour

Responsibility vs. fate related idiomatic expressions—

At fault	Knock oneself out
Beat around the bush	Make the best of
Bring off	Nothing succeeds like success
By chance	Press one's luck
By oneself	Put all one's eggs in one
Free hand/free rein	basket
Go out of one's way	Put one's best foot forward
Have a hand in	Roll up one's sleeves
Have it coming	See to it
Help oneself	Serve one right
Hold one's own	Stand a chance
In charge (of)	Take a chance
In luck	Take charge
In one's way	Take upon oneself
In the face of	To blame
Keep one's fingers crossed	To no avail
Knock on wood	Under the circumstances

Consider each of the following three dialogues. The idiomatic expressions are italicized. Then the same conversation takes place without the use of idioms. In negotiating with Japanese businessmen it is important to avoid idiomatic expressions as much as possible, although it is difficult.

Situation One

A meeting has just been called for all department managers to discuss "X" company's main competitor's introduction of a product improvement which threatens their share of the market.

Manager A: Well, it looks like we really got *caught with our pants down* this time!

Manager B: Maybe not. "Z" may have *let the cat out of the bag* a little too soon. With some effort, we may be able to *cash in on* their mistake.

Manager A: Oh come now. We've got a lot *at stake* here. We've always *set the pace* in this industry, and now "Z" is threatening *to take over*.

Manager B: I admit that it will be *touch and go* for awhile, but if we *roll up our sleeves* and *get a move on* we won't *lose* any more *ground*.

Manager A: But R&D has always had ample lead time for product development. We can't just ask them to *throw something together on the spur of the moment*. That would be *out of line* with our corporate image, and would hurt us *in the long run* as well.

Manager B: Well I am sure that R&D is *on top of* the situation. Let's call them in and have them *point out* our options.

Without idioms—

Manager A: Well, it seems we were caught unprepared this time.

Manager B: Maybe not. "Z" may have exposed their secret development too quickly. With some effort, we may be able to take advantage of their mistake.

Manager A: We have a lot to lose. We've always been the leader in this industry. Now "Z" is threatening to take our place.

Manager B: I admit it will be precarious for awhile, but if we begin immediately to work hard together we won't be delayed further.

Manager A: But R&D has always had ample lead time for product development. We can't just ask them to participate without adequate preparation. That would not agree with our company image, and would hurt us in the future.

Manager B: Well, I'm sure that R&D can manage the situation. Let's call them in and have them identify our options.

Situation Two

Managers A and B meet with R&D management. After being fully briefed on the project status, the following conversation takes place:

Manager A: What it *all boils down to,* then, is that if we incorporate the "Z" type improvement into our current production, at least we won't *have to rule out* keeping everything *on schedule.*

Manager B: Yes, our product readily *lends itself to* the improvement, and we can manage the change without *taking any* big chances.

Manager A: Well, *under the circumstances,* I think we should *take advantage* of that little bit of good fortune and *see to it* that R&D *gets on it right away.* You know, *time is money.* . . .

Manager B: Yes, but I'd like to *point out* that the new design improvement which we've had scheduled to go on line soon shouldn't be *put to bed* just to compete with "Z."

Manager A: I'm not *reading* you very *clearly.* If you *have something on your mind,* please *get to the point.*

Manager B: If we *jump the gun* and come out now with a "Z" type improvement, we'd just be *playing catch-up.* But if we *bide our time* until we can introduce both improvements in a new model early next year, the *long run effect* will very likely be positive.

Manager A: I *have had it* with all this talk of waiting and catching up. If it is up to me to *call the shots,* I won't let "Z" *edge* us *out* of our position even in the short run. After all, we are *number one* and will stay number one.

Manager B: Well, we should *make the best of* this situation. Let's take *time out* to consider where we stand *on the whole.* Shall we *take five?*

Without idioms—

Manager A: Basically then, if we incorporate the "Z" type improvement into our current production, at least we will be able to keep everything going as planned.

Manager B: Yes, our product can easily be improved, and we can manage without risking failure.

Manager A: Well, in this situation, we can make good use of our good fortune and make sure that R&D begins immediately. You know, we may lose money if we take too much time . . .

Manager B: Yes, but I'd like to mention that the new design improvement that we've had scheduled to begin soon shouldn't be eliminated just to compete with "Z."

Manager A: I don't understand you very well. If you are thinking about something, please tell me what you're thinking.

Manager B: If we act too quickly without thinking and come out with a "Z" type improvement, we'd always be behind trying to reach "Z," never to overtake them. But if we wait patiently until we can introduce both improvements in a new model early next year, the eventual effect will very likely be positive.

Manager A: I'm tired of all this talk of waiting and catching up. If it is up to me to give the orders, I won't let

"Z" take our place even briefly. After all, we're the best and we'll stay the best.

Manager B: Well, we should do as much as we can with this situation and not complain. Let's stop to consider our overall position. Shall we take a break?

Situation Three

The meeting has been reconvened and alternatives discussed. Meeting conclusion and adjournment:

Manager A: I believe we are finally *on top of* things now. I am pleased that you *put your foot down* and decided to *take charge.*

Manager B: Well, I am convinced that we can *kill two birds with one stone* by combining both improvements, even if we *take into account* that it will take awhile longer than we'd like.

Manager A: I don't think it is *out of the question* that we'll be able to use this situation to our advantage. If we *carry out* the plan exactly as we discussed it and *hold the line* on costly changes, we should be *out of the woods in no time.*

Manager B: Well, *so far, so good.* Let's *wrap it up* and *call it a day.* I'll have the formal plan on your desk at 9:00 *on the dot,* even if I have to write it up *by myself.*

Without idioms—

Manager A: I believe we are finally in control of things now. I am pleased you intervened and decided to undertake the management of the project.

Manager B: Well, I am convinced that we can succeed in two things through one action, if we combine both improvements, even if we consider that it will take longer than we'd like.

Manager A: It is not impossible that we'll be able to use this situation to our advantage. If we implement the plan exactly as we discussed it and control the costly changes, we should be out of trouble very soon.

Manager B: Well, we've made good progress. Let's finish for today. I'll have the formal plan on your desk at 9:00 punctually, even if I have to write it up personally.

American businessmen are aware of the difficulty involved in learning a foreign language, especially the idiomatic expressions. It is important that as American negotiators, we take great care when speaking with Japanese negotiators by being aware that the English language, like many languages, is made up in large part of slang and idiomatic expressions that native speakers take for granted. We must be sensitized to this and realize that even "fluent" nonnative speakers may not understand the concepts implied in these expressions.

Because a negotiating counterpart may appear to have a good command of our language, we cannot assume that everything we say will be interpreted in the way we intend it to be.

Using Interpreters

The Japanese have a joke that goes,

Q: "What do you call a person who can speak two languages?"
A: "Bilingual."
Q: "How about three?"
A: "Trilingual."
Q: "Good, how about one?"
A: "Hmmm . . . American!"

The importance of an interpreter in business negotiations cannot be overstressed. It is the interpreter who can assist with the accurate communication of ideas between the two teams. It

is advisable to remember the following points concerning the
use of interpreters:

- [ ] Brief the interpreter in advance about the subject. (Select an interpreter knowledgeable about the product, if possible.)
- [ ] Speak clearly and slowly.
- [ ] Avoid little-known words, such as "arcane" or "heuristic."
- [ ] Explain a major idea two or three different ways, as the point may be lost if discussed only once.
- [ ] Do not talk more than a minute or two without giving the interpreter a chance to speak.
- [ ] While talking, allow the interpreter time to make notes of what is being said.
- [ ] Assume that all numbers over 10,000 may be mistranslated. Repeat them carefully and write them down for all to see. The Japanese system of counting large numbers is different from that of the West, and errors frequently occur.
- [ ] Do not lose confidence if the interpreter uses a dictionary.
- [ ] Permit the interpreter to spend as much time as needed in clarifying points whose meanings are obscure.
- [ ] Do not interrupt the interpreter as he translates, as interrupting causes many misunderstandings.
- [ ] Avoid long sentences, double negatives, or the use of negative wordings of a sentence when a positive form could be used.
- [ ] Avoid superfluous words. Your point may be lost if wrapped up in generalities.
- [ ] Try to be expressive and use gestures to support your verbal messages.
- [ ] During meetings, write out the main points discussed. In this way both parties can double check their understanding.
- [ ] After meetings, confirm in writing what has been agreed.
- [ ] Don't expect an interpreter to work for over two hours without a rest period.
- [ ] Consider using two interpreters if interpreting is to last a

whole day or into the evening, so that when one tires the other can take over.

☐ Don't be concerned if a speaker talks for five minutes and the interpreter covers it in half a minute.

☐ Be understanding if it develops that the interpreter has made a mistake. Japanese and European languages are very dissimilar.

☐ Be sure the Japanese are given all the time they want to tell their side of the story. If they hesitate, ask the interpreter for advice on what next to say or do.

☐ Interpreting English into Japanese takes longer (1.5 times) than vice versa.

After the Negotiation

After the negotiation session, arrange to spend time with the interpreter. The interpreter is culturally sensitive to the Japanese and can be used as a sort of post meeting guide. The interpreter could have noticed important details that may have escaped the attention of persons not fully aware of the Japanese system.

There are a variety of things that may go wrong, but if the interpreter is used to his fullest advantage, there is no reason for mistakes to repeat themselves.

7

The Negotiating Session

Negotiation in Japan: A Case

*T*he following is based on the experiences of several Americans and illustrates what can happen when negotiating with the Japanese.

Free Enterprises, Inc. is a multinational producer of soaps and cosmetic products with 50% of sales in foreign markets. They distribute overseas through exclusive and nonexclusive distributorships, and have marketing subsidiaries established in Europe and Hong Kong. The product is standardized for sale overseas, but the brand name, packaging, and promotion are adapted to suit particular regional markets.

Fumio Limited is a major trading company in Tokyo that handles a complete line of commodities including nonprescription pharmaceuticals, cleaning products, and cosmetics.

R. J. Bennett, vice-president of Asian sales for Free Enterprises prepared a proposal to enter the Japanese market, largely based on research done on sales projections and market potential. The advantages to entering the Japanese market were primarily those of opening up a new market with a large profit potential. There were concerns about the expense involved in adapting packaging for the market and the degree of competition already present, especially in the area of cosmetics.

The initial contact between the two companies was correspondence between Steve Dobbs, the director and vice-president of Asian sales, and Y. Tanaka, director of foreign affairs (*bucho*) for Fumio for six months. At Fumio, there is an exchange of information concerning Free Enterprises' proposal among the various departments (nonprescription pharmaceuticals, finance, quality) and the proposal to initiate preliminary negotiations is approved by senior management. Fumio is impressed by Enterprises' domestic and foreign operations, the quality of their products, and the products' potential appeal in the Japanese market. They consider added expense in storage facilities, warehouse personnel, and the strong competition in the cosmetics market before making a decision. The invitation for preliminary negotiations is sent by Tanaka to Dobbs with a request for a tentative agenda. The agenda is sent, revised, and returned within eight weeks.

Free Enterprises appoints Dobbs to head the negotiation team. He is young, ambitious, well-educated with an MBA from a prestigious university, and has worked for a trading company in Hong Kong, though he has limited experience in the Japanese market. The Japanese account would increase his duties and prestige in the company considerably. A letter of introduction is sent by the president of the company and Bennett, the vice-president of Asian sales.

Dobbs flies to Japan alone, expecting to be joined by his colleagues in the latter phases of the negotiations. He meets with the director of foreign affairs, Tanaka, who refers him to the manager of pharmaceuticals (*kacho*) S. Abe, who in turn refers him down to the section chief (*shunin*) in charge of nonprescription pharmaceuticals, K. Oonishi. During this week-long process, Dobbs is well received and has many pleasant conversational exchanges, but has difficulty setting a specific date for the first session. He is frustrated and calls Bennett, who sends a telex to the general manager outlining more specifically Dobb's qualifications and authority to negotiate for Free Enterprises. After several more informal meetings, Dobbs receives a call that establishes a time for the first session the following day.

Tanaka, K. Oonishi and K. Yamaguchi, the section chief in charge of new accounts in the finance division, meet with staff and later among themselves in a preliminary session. They cover points in the agenda and have a good idea from several experiences dealing with American companies what they intend to offer in terms of price and distribution arrangements.

Bill Smith, senior sales coordinator of Asian sales (who has been with the company for twenty years, previously having been a successful salesman, and is very familiar with the Enterprise product line), and John Manning, director of inventory control, fly out to help with the presentation and negotiation at the request of Bennett, who is beginning to worry about Dobb's chances for success on his own.

A letter of invitation from Tanaka is sent to the American team along with a copy of the revised agenda. The conference room at Fumio is set up with a large table with seating for each team on either side. Audiovisual equipment is available and service facilities for tea and coffee are present.

The Japanese team is led by Tanaka who has with him his assistant, M. Kato. K. Oonishi, department chief of nonprescription pharamaceuticals, is present with his assistant, K. Tokunaga, the general manager of the warehouse (section chief status). M. Sotomura and K. Yamaguchi, who are in charge of new accounts, are also present.

The American team enters the room and the Japanese team forms a line to greet them. Tanaka shakes hands with Dobbs and the rest follow suit, introducing themselves. The Americans bow slightly and shake hands. The Japanese are dressed in dark, conservative suits. The Americans are dressed in stylish light blue, navy, and grey two-piece suits. Business cards are exchanged and the Americans have come prepared with cards printed in Japanese and English. Two of the Americans make the mistake of handing their cards upside down. The Japanese team takes the cards and places them on the table in front of them. The Americans place the cards in their portfolios. The Japanese have brought an interpreter, M. Sumida. The team leaders sit down first, and the rest follow.

Dobbs is invited to open for his team, and he makes some courteous remarks. The Americans are surprised when the assistant, M. Kato, responds with opening remarks in reasonably good English. Tanaka states a few sentences in faltering English. As the courtesies continue for close to an hour, the Americans feel obliged to be very polite in turn but are getting restless.

Dobbs decides to take charge of the situation and introduces Smith, who is scheduled to make a two-and-one-half-hour presentation of Free Enterprises, Inc., which includes brochures and slides. Smith has made this presentation before, but never with an interpreter. He has difficulty pausing for translation and rushes through the presentation without adequate question periods. He also uses many numerical figures which seem to confuse the interpreter. At the end of his presentation, Smith's call for questions is met with a long, awkward silence. The Japanese chain smoke and talk among themselves. The interpreter is asked if there are any misunderstandings, and he mentions something to a member of the team. After more discussion, Oonishi asks a question concerning some recent downward trends in sales in Latin America that were not mentioned. Smith is not very familiar with Latin American operations but promises to provide the information at the following meeting. Oonishi's assistant then makes a request for some recent trade publication articles on Free Enterprises' operations in Asia and a loan of the slide presentation to show other departments in the company. Again, Smith promises to procure the information and lend the slides. The Japanese seem satisfied with his response but give no further feedback. They talk among themselves a short while longer and are quiet.

Tanaka's assistant, M. Kato, gives a presentation of Fumio, Limited, which includes a history of the corporation and its current distribution system in Japan. He also mentions some of the company's prestigious distributors and how Fumio services them. His presentation includes a slide show and many handouts and commercial portfolios. Using a translator, although he can speak English well, Kato reads from a prepared speech, looking at his notes frequently or looking past the conference participants. A question-and-answer session follows.

A review of the agenda items follows. Dobbs decides to pursue some major, potentially controversial issues in order to establish a forum for future discussion. Among these are the concerns about Enterprises' reputation for speedy delivery and compensation for damaged goods. Dobbs starts proposing methods and systems for estimating shipping time and developing a formula for compensation. When he asks for a response, he receives a seemingly vague answer from Sotomura, who says that he is sure that whatever is worked out will be equitable to both parties. Dobbs pursues the issue but realizes from nonverbal cues (Tanaka and Oonishi lean back in their seats and are seemingly resistant) that the topic is unwelcome and drops it.

Dobbs completes a summary of the agenda without delving into any of the topics. There is one minor clarification of the wording of a point but no discussion of the agenda as a whole. The Japanese team requests a break. When they all return, the Japanese request a continuation of the session the following day. They also invite the Americans out to dinner at a restaurant that evening.

At dinner, the teams have an opportunity to meet informally. The Americans are a bit awkward with the food and make nervous, joking comments. Dobbs is a bit put off when Tanaka inquires about his ethnic background and religion; he answers, but is guarded. Smith asks for feedback on the proposal and receives a positive response, which he takes to mean that they agree to the key issues at hand. The Americans at one point lightly criticize U.S. government policies toward business and are met with silence. In general, Dobbs is feeling positive and calls Bennett that night. He tells him he is sure he will not have to come down far from his original offer and the deal will be "wrapped up" in a week. He tells the home office to draw up a rough draft of the contract.

The Japanese team has altered slightly. Yamaguchi has left for several sessions and two marketing specialists from pharmaceuticals have joined the team. Smith has brought product samples, brochures and, specifications. He goes through a great deal of material, describing the product line in detail, stressing the qualities of the biggest selling product, "Dewdrop" soap, and describing its history of success in the domestic and foreign markets. He uses the hard sell approach that made him successful as a salesman, stressing each need and benefit for the Japanese market. Dobbs presents a handout of sales projections for Japan. The Americans by this time have hired and briefed their own interpreter who busily looks up some of the more difficult words in the dictionary. Dobbs wonders if they have chosen a competent interpreter.

The Japanese are concerned about the sales projections. They wonder if they are realistic and want to see the information sources. During one of the question-and-answer periods, K. Tokunaga stands up and begins to discuss life in Japan, particularly the types of cleaning products that Japanese consumers use. Smith is confused as to the nature of the discourse and interrupts, asking for clarification but not waiting for a response. He starts to highlight the major attributes of the product line once again. He adds more evidence as to sales projections. A long period of silence ensues. Smith notices Tanaka puts his hands together, covering his mouth. Dobbs breaks the silence and asks directly for any recommendations for product modifications in the Japanese market. Kato makes a halting response by asking about consumer use of cleaning products in America and how these relate to the American lifestyle. He also asks Dobbs how he thinks this lifestyle differs from the European lifestyle. Dobbs is considerably confused and frustrated. He takes off his jacket, loosens his tie, leans back and crosses his legs as he thinks of his next move. He decides to request a break to confer.

After the break, Manning discusses the distribution system in the U.S. and expresses concern over the capability of Japanese retailers to handle Enterprises' full line of cosmetics because of the limited shelf life of certain products. He uses expressions such as "walk through" meaning special orders that need to be walked through the system, "lead time," and "pick up," which the interpreter has a difficult time translating. More difficulties in communication ensue because the Japanese, especially Sotomura, believe that the Americans want them to make significant changes in their distribution system just to accommodate Enterprises' products. The Americans, however, were discussing the feasibility of introducing certain products into the system right away because of the risk of limited shelf life. The session ends with Sotomura attempting to explain the unique nature of the Japanese distribution system and how difficult it is for foreigners to understand this system, since it is so particularly suited to Japan. The group leaves to take a tour of Fumio's warehouse facilities.

For the next two weeks Dobbs has difficulty in scheduling another session. The pressure from the home office is increasing
as the negotiations have lasted much longer than expected and
they have not reached an agreement on even minor points in the
contract.

Dobbs suggests that Smith talk to Kato because of his profi-
ciency in English and his connection to Tanaka. Smith makes
several "informal" visits, and they enter into generally nonbusi-
ness oriented discussions. Kato finally suggests in an indirect
fashion a visit to Sotomura. Smith begins to learn some of the
concerns that the Japanese have regarding the contract. They
are concerned about the long-term risk involved in carrying the
product in terms of the limited five-year contract that has been
proposed, and they wonder about the validity of the information
sources upon which the Americans based their sales projections
in the Japanese market. The Japanese feel that they need more
time to study the market analysis. In addition, to make any modifications in the distribution system would require a substantial
financial investment.

The Americans receive another call to set up an additional
round of sessions. More information, (including cables and correspondence from the home office during the negotiation period) is requested. The Americans are prepared to address most
of the concerns but basically interpret the crisis as "holding
cost" and adjust their positions on price, delivery time, and volume.

A major controversy continues to be compensation for damaged goods. Dobbs suggests a 60–40 split, down from his original request of 100% compensation. K. Tokunaga mentions that
with the amount of service that Fumio is providing, there should
be no need for setting a percentage for damaged goods.

The Japanese do not understand the need for Enterprises to
plan for an uncertain event so specifically and on such a long-
term basis. Manning starts throwing out prices and volumes, his
interpreter is having problems keeping up. He continues to receive little reaction from the Japanese team.

Dobbs decides to leave "damaged goods" and go over points
in the contract that he believes have been agreed upon up to this
point. One concerns delivery time from the minutes of previous

meetings. Dobbs points out a specific delivery time that he assumed was agreed upon by both parties. The Japanese seem confused and begin to talk among themselves. Dobbs asks the interpreter for assistance. It turns out to be a problem of mistranslation and misinterpretation of key concepts. The Japanese considered their affirmation to be an intent to keep to a certain range of time, not a specific delivery time. Dobbs becomes unnerved and shows his anger when he insists that they had agreed upon that point. The negotiators seem to have hit another snag.

Preliminary Activities

Initial Contacts

In Japan initial contacts are very formal and the Japanese negotiators keep their distance until they have reached a business agreement. It is often a long time before an actual negotiation session can be arranged. For example, if an American businessman flies to Japan alone, he should expect a lengthy visit to the Japanese firm before an actual negotiation session can be arranged. The Japanese view this as a time to establish a relationship with the company and a time to discuss anything from your golf handicap to the products of your company. An American businessman can also expect many formal and informal meetings with many corporate employees ranging from the vice-president to director of foreign relations to the department chief and his assistants. These meetings are a critical point in establishing a lasting relationship with the negotiating team.

When an American businessman is alone to conduct business meetings or negotiations, the Japanese may perceive that his company is not serious about conducting business. To avoid such a situation, the businessman should always have a letter of introduction sent to the Japanese firm before his arrival stating that he has the authority to negotiate in place of a high corporate executive. However, it would be advantageous to send more than one individual to conduct these opening sessions with the Japanese firm. For example, if you were attempting to negotiate a product distribution contract with a Japanese trading firm, you should include those individuals who are directly concerned with this proposal, mainly inventory control, regional sales, and perhaps even the product marketer.

Negotiation Room and Seating

An American businessman can expect much of the same modern furniture in Japanese offices as in the United States. The typical negotiation room consists of a rectangular table with chairs on either side and perhaps chairs at each end of the table. Generally, the seating arrangements are informal in that there are no assigned seats, but the Japanese are usually on one side of the table and the Americans on the other. The Japanese make their preference known, and the team leaders sit across from one another. When formal presentations are necessary, they are conducted by the team leaders or the technical people.

Often, the seats on both ends of the negotiating table are reserved for the interpreters of both teams and any secretary who may be taking notes.

Business Cards

It is important that business cards be exchanged at the first formal meeting session. American businessmen should acquire business cards that are bilingual—English on one side and Japanese on the other. This service is provided by most hotels in Japan and usually takes only about 24 hours. Upon presenting the business card, the card should be given to the Japanese so that they are able to read your name and position with the company. This carries great weight with the Japanese in that they wish to know who you are and with what area of the company your efforts are most concerned. Generally, the card is presented to the Japanese accompanied by a nod or bow. The Japanese use these cards as a form of reference when you are speaking.

The Japanese negotiating team often has more members than the foreign team. The Japanese may be at a "low-key" priority level as far as doing business with your firm at this time.

They are still gathering facts, still researching the alternatives and most of all, attempting to build the relationship as the negotiation session continues. There probably will be either an addition to the number of Japanese on the team or a continuous transition of individuals. This is because the Japanese are serious about making a contract with your firm and are involving as many individuals as needed to make the decision.

Telephones will be present in the room with many Japanese being called to the telephone during the session. Coffee, tea, and Japanese tea are served routinely.

Making a Presentation

A striking feature about the Japanese is their desire to know as much as they can about your firm. From the moment your firm contacts their firm, you can assume they have begun a thorough investigation of your firm.

Be prepared to answer some general and detailed questions about your firm's activities, short-comings, and long-term objectives. For example, upon completing a presentation about your company's objectives in Japan, you should not be shocked when your Japanese counterpart requests to know more about a recent sales slump in your company's Latin American market. Obviously, this has nothing to do with your objectives in Japan, but the Japanese are not just concerned with those objectives alone. They want to know how your company reacts to uncertainties, how secure your firm's record has been overall to its foreign operations, and most of all, how this could perhaps relate to them in the future.

Audiovisual aids such as graphs, charts, and films are recommended. Also, handouts can be very helpful, especially when there are language difficulties. This gives the Japanese a chance to provide additional information to other individuals involved in the decision-making. If you wish to use a film or slide presentation, be prepared to offer the use of this presentation to the Japanese so that they might show this to the other individuals not at the meeting. Audiovisual material also demonstrates seriousness and sincerity in negotiating.

If an extended moment of silence occurs during a meeting, do not assume they disapprove of your statements or that they were not listening. This period of silence is normally a time of reflection on what was said. It is also a gesture of respect to the speaker. If you have any questions, write them down and ask them when the speaker has finished. Frequently interrupting the speaker is considered rude and could damage a business relationship between the Japanese and you.

During the negotiation, there will be breaks or pauses in the discussions. During these periods, it is advisable to review points that were covered in the previous sessions or discuss among your teammates the progress and direction of your objectives. This time may also be utilized to further inform the interpreter of the meeting or to get a clarification on some points discussed in the presentation.

Much time is spent in conferences because the Japanese desire thorough explanations of every point; and they use these meetings to size up their counterparts and establish the necessary relationship desired in order to conduct business. They spend a lot of time studying the personalities of those around them and compare notes with one another.

It is recommended that one person on the American team take notes during the meetings. These can be typed and distributed to the other members for discussion and summarization.

At the Negotiating Table

Guidelines for Cultural Awareness

Cultural perceptions of negotiating procedures differ widely in Japan and the United States and it is helpful to recognize how styles differ in order to achieve harmonious and productive business relationships during negotiations.

The Japanese are closely attuned to the cyclical nature of events and are very aware of the uncertainty that the future holds. The Japanese, although very formal in their processes, are also cognizant of the gap between formality and reality, realizing that in practice, transactions are never so simple as they appear on paper. They incorporate a certain degree of flexibility in their business dealings, such as with agendas and contracts.

The Japanese also have a great sense of personal honor and believe a commitment is an intention to carry through to the best of one's abilities. If someone, during the long process of negotiating sessions, is judged trustworthy or sincere, there does not exist a great need to spell out detailed responsibilities. A good approach is to avoid bargaining on minor points but develop a formula by which both sides can benefit from instead of each point being either a "win" or "concession." Toward the end of a negotiation, there is often a great deal of silent concentrated effort of reaching a harmonious consensus. Americans can feel uneasy and interpret that something has "gone wrong" or that they have been misunderstood. A last ditch effort may be made unnecessarily that can destroy progress that has been accomplished.

Managing a Crisis

At some point during the negotiations, a crisis usually arises. Negotiations may be broken and the prospects of a successful conclusion dim. This situation could last a few days to several weeks, but it is important to keep the communication channels open. This can be accomplished by discreetly asking lower-level executives and managers about who is opposing the deal and why. These individuals, with their company's best interest foremost, will offer suggestions as to how to approach this difficulty. If the Japanese president or some other high officer is in favor of the proposal, he may arrange for a private luncheon at which the opponents of the plan will explain their views to the visitors. A process of "selling one's face" could also be exercised whereby the businessman will drop in on his "nay-sayer" counterpart for a casual talk from time to time without making an appointment. This may have to be repeated several times before things can get moving ahead in a positive manner again.

The use of a third party is also a common practice. It usually involves asking a mutual friend or business associate to find out what the problem is. The chances of success can be further enforced if the go-between is a member of the same club or group as the opponent, or is an alumnus of the same university or high school. If such is the case, the go-between is likely to have considerable influence.

A crisis period occasionally results in conflict on the Japanese team because the individual opposing the proposal is not "pressured" into agreeing, and until the conflict can be resolved, the Japanese tend to leave it as it is rather than make a decision.

Some suggestions to keep in mind during a negotiating session:

- □ Don't get too involved with details of the contract too early in the session. The Japanese may feel that the details can be worked out as the relationship continues to grow.
- □ Try not to use an aggressive approach to selling your idea. Japanese feel that your idea or product should speak for itself. A low-key approach is better.
- □ Don't interrupt when someone is speaking. This is considered rude by most Japanese.
- □ Try to be formal. Do not ask if it would be O.K. to call them by their first names or if everyone can take off their suit coats to relax. This type of atmosphere or approach tends to give the Japanese a feeling of a lack of sincerity.
- □ Always bring as much information as possible about your plans and your firm. Published articles are of great advantage.
- □ Better not to approach the Japanese alone. Send a group (two or three) to conduct the negotiations. This is a sign of earnestness to the Japanese. Make certain you send the appropriate individuals who can make the decisions.
- □ Do not demand an immediate decision on points covered in the meetings. As most decisions are made in groups, the Japanese team needs time to compare notes and discuss matters.
- □ Do not be offended if the Japanese tend to inquire about your religious or political beliefs. These are common questions used in Japan because they are interested in knowing as much about you and your company as possible. It is a confidence builder.

☐ If you get stuck on a point, don't continue to beat away on it. Move on to other points and come back when the other team has had time to think about it.

☐ Keep reviewing those points that were agreed upon during the meeting, trying to move forward in a constructive manner.

☐ Maintain good communications with your interpreter. The interpreter may be able to inform you on the progress of the contract or perhaps possible conflicts that may be avoided.

☐ Speak slowly and with patience. Do not rattle off numbers to indicate your knowledge of the project. Numbers can be studied in detail by the Japanese at a later date.

☐ Be prepared for misunderstandings and clarify the points with sincerity and a willingness to assist.

☐ Don't cover difficult points first on the agenda. Work toward a common ground, but be flexible enough to realize that ground may totally change before the contract is signed.

Evaluating Progress

It is helpful to spend some time analyzing a session with members of your team, using a checklist or questionnaire. Review your session notes, carefully noting any inconsistencies or misinterpretations of key issues. Remember reactions of the Japanese team, particularly towards each other during discussions or presentations. When you evaluate your perceptions, consider:

☐ Communications styles and barriers to effective communication, such as differences between Japanese and American business ethics and practices, general cultural guidelines, stereotypical views, and limited experience with members of the other culture.

☐ Conflict resolution—How do you as a group resolve conflicts that come up during a session? How do the Japanese work as a team in reaching consensus?

☐ Decision-making techniques—What are the methods of decision making utilized by your team? Does one person make all the major decisions? Does majority rule when a consensus is reached? How does the method affect each side's viewing of the negotiation process? Are the decisions based in part on "rational" linear thinking and/or intuition?

☐ Leadership styles—Who are the leaders of each team, and how do they interact with the other team members? Do they "take over" or delegate responsibility? Do they listen to subordinates and follow their suggestions? Do they exert a strong, calming influence or do they tend to be more on the charismatic, motivationally enthusiastic side?

Above all, remember the contrast in motivations from the point of view of both sides. What does each side stand to gain or lose from the outcome? Do not assume that the other team is there for exactly the same reasons.

Synergy, Not Compromise

Synergy is basically a model of interaction between two individuals or organizations from different cultural settings. A good example that has become quite popular recently is the type Z organization whereby American firms are using aspects of Japanese management style with success in an American cultural context. Synergy is taking values, techniques, and principles from two cultures and combining them to elevate the whole to a higher level of efficiency and harmony. Compromise is give and take, which reinforces the assumption of a "win-lose" proposition. Synergy is "win-win", nothing is given up or lost. It requires much sensitivity and understanding on the part of participants, but is certainly achievable. For example, in a negotiating session between an American and a Japanese firm concerning shipping times and the delivery of goods, the Americans may desire a specific deadline for delivery due to the security and consistency of having time frames on paper. The Japanese do not wish to commit themselves to specific deadlines which, if not met, would cause a problem. The synergistic solution may be to specify a range of times for the delivery date. This solution would satisfy the American's desire to see something written into the contract and allow the Japanese some flexibility in case something delayed the shipment.

The next chapter addresses entertainment, an important aspect of doing business in Japan.

8

Entertainment

*I*n negotiating with Japanese businessmen, many Americans, under pressure from the home office, try to get the Japanese to make quick decisions. Since this is typically not the Japanese way of doing business, and entertainment is a large part of the "negotiating waltz," the American businessman would be well-advised to acquaint himself with this aspect of business.

The personal nature of the Japanese business system makes close, trusting interpersonal relations as or more important to the Japanese than favorable business terms. To the Japanese, the total business relationship is based on many personal factors, and maintaining harmonious relationships that involve mutual trust and help now and in the future take precedence over profit.

To this end, you should familiarize yourself with the various settings for entertainment, and certain customs and etiquette observed in those settings.

Bars and Cabarets

The "hosutesu baa" (hostess bar) figures prominently in Japanese business, and it is often viewed as the recreational wing of "Japan, Inc." In Tokyo alone, there are over 50,000 of them with many of the fancier ones in nightlife centers such as the Ginza, Akasaka, and Roppongi. They are customarily small, intimate, and expensive. A routine night out for four in one of the better places could easily cost $300–$500. The standard practice is to purchase a "keep" bottle of whiskey which, depending on the brand will cost between 5,000 and 25,000 yen ($25–$125). This bottle is then kept on the premises, ready to be consumed on demand. One is assessed a "table charge" per visit, which is the Japanese equivalent of a cover charge. There is also the bottled mineral water and ice charge. In addition, there is a charge, at varying rates per hour, for the hostesses assigned to you. They will also help to fatten the bill by prevailing on you to buy them drinks at inflated prices.

How do the Japanese tolerate this? How can they afford to come to these places on a regular basis? Much of the sting of the bill is taken out considering that almost all Japanese executives come equipped with hefty expense accounts. The company entertainment fee is tax deductible and the amount is determined by the company annual sales volume. Secondly, the Japanese businessman chooses his bars with care, and will only patronize a few favorites. He will have close, friendly relationships with the female manager of each place (fondly calling her "mama") and a few favorite hostesses. The cabarets strive to provide an atmosphere in which each individual customer can escape from the daily routine of his structured life and enjoy himself. The hostess will, at different times, pamper, tease, and counsel her patrons. She is there to make them laugh, make them forget themselves, and give them a woman's loving attention. In the midst of all of this, it is little wonder that the Japanese will cheerfully part with bags of yen to avail themselves of these services. It is her business to encourage amorous rapport with *all* her customers.

Another place for entertainment is reserved for the V.I.P.'s of Japanese companies—bank presidents or managing directors of large corporations. These places are called *clubs,* with the individual name following (e.g., Club Jun). Basically the same as hostess bars, they feature professional live entertainment and the most beautiful, intelligent, and charming hostesses to be found. If you are not soon invited to one by a Japanese and consider a nonexpense account visit, remember that most are "members only," and all will require you to part with a minimum of 100,000 yen per person ($500).

Scotch and water, known as *mizuwari* in Japanese, is the overwhelming favorite of Japanese drinkers. Japan's scotch consumption per capita is the highest in the world. As previously mentioned, Japanese maintain a "keep" bottle of their favorite scotch in the bars and desire to impress their guests—it may be a bottle of Japan's most popular scotch, Suntory Old or Chivas Regal. If beer is preferred, more than likely you will be served Kirin, the most popular beer in Japan, with a 70% market share. Other domestic Japanese beers (there are only four) are Sapporo, Suntory, and Asahi. Sake (pronounced "sahkay" not "sacky") is the Japanese national alcoholic beverage. It is fermented rice wine, usually served warm (at 98°F) and best taken in small doses. (A word of caution: you can easily lose track of how much sake you consumed, and a sake hangover is of Godzilla-sized proportions.)

For Japanese, drinking together is a logical extension of their affinity for group effort and teamwork. All members of a party will drink from the same bottle. Beer comes in 633 ml (21-oz) bottles and is never served individually or drunk from the bottle. It is considered impolite to allow a fellow group member to mix his own drink or pour his own beer or sake. A very common and important way of establishing rapport and good relations with a Japanese is to fix a drink for him, and then offer a toast by touching glasses and saying *kampai* (cheers). To be polite, he will immediately attempt to refill your own glass and initiate his own *kampai*. (When having your drink filled, it is considered good etiquette to reach out and raise your glass.) This scene will be repeated throughout the evening, forging closer personal relations through a shared experience.

Japan has extremely strict drunk-driver laws, and Japanese businessmen will either go home by taxi, chauffered car, or train.

Karaoke

At some point during your night out, you will be in a bar that has a *karaoke* set up (almost all hostess bars and clubs have them). *Karaoke* literally means "empty orchestra" and are recordings of popular songs with the vocal part deleted. Every popular Japanese song imaginable is recorded on 8-track tapes, without a singer. The words of all the songs are contained in several looseleaf binders. Many Japanese are accomplished singers, and most Japanese businessmen find it socially expedient to have a few favorite songs ready to go when required to take center stage. One simply tells the hostess the title of the song, and readies the words in front of him. The person is then handed a microphone, the tape is started, and everyone in the bar is serenaded with a live performance. Everyone in the group is called upon to sing at least one number. This is an excellent way of being drawn into and establishing closer social ties with the group of Japanese you are dealing with. They will unquestionably appreciate the effort in overcoming your embarrassment and taking part in a wholly Japanese custom. It is another mutually shared experience in which your participation can and will be gauged by your Japanese counterparts.

Food

In Tokyo, there are any number of Western restaurants specializing in food familiar to anyone's palate. When being taken out for dinner, your Japanese host will usually first inquire as to whether you would prefer Western or Oriental cuisine. If you stick with Western food, you will suffer no surprises, but you will miss an excellent opportunity to show your interest in the Japanese culture, and a willingness to try things Japanese. In addition, you will be passing up some delightful and utterly delicious fare.

Apart from Benihana-style prepared steak, there are three types of Japanese food that are very popular and very palatable to a Westerner's taste.

Tempura—An assortment of vegetables, shrimp, and scallops dipped in a light batter, quickly deep-fried in oil, and eaten with a delicious slightly sweet tempura sauce.

Beef Sukiyaki—An all-time favorite, it consists of thin strips of beef, mushrooms, and other vegetables cooked in front of you in a soup made from soy sauce, sugar, and sake. Rice is served with it, and also a raw egg (not mandatory).

Shabu-shabu—Thin, top-quality slices of beef are swirled around a pot of boiling water for a second or two to just barely cook it, and then eaten. The broth created by cooking the beef in the water is then used to make a stew.

Any of these dishes can be eaten without any qualms of being forced to ingest any strange creature from the sea or secret herbs. In fact, the more familiar you become with Japanese cuisine the more you will find almost all of it eminently delicious. For Westerners who like fish, sushi is an ideal dish.

Sushi—What is sushi? It is *not* slimy, malodorous, bloody chunks of raw fish, which seems to be the impression of many Westerners. It is a slice of fish on a small mound of rice with a dab of Japanese horseradish (*wasabi*) in between. Only the highest quality rice is used, and it is cooked and seasoned with vinegar, salt, and sugar. Sushi shops only use the choicest parts from the freshest fish, so the fish never has an unpleasant odor nor is it unsafe to eat. Pieces of sushi are mouth-sized and can be picked up with either chopsticks or your hand. There are several kinds and styles of sushi, the most popular using tuna, eel, shrimp, mackerel, and shellfish. Not all the fish is raw; some is boiled, some is cooked, and some is marinated. Also there are sushi made with egg omelets and certain vegetables for those wishing a gradual initiation.

Conversation

Now that you are in a social setting and developing good personal relations, the time has come to engage in conversation that you hope will prove you to be a sincere, interesting person whom they can trust and would desire closer business ties with. Although many American businessmen who have worked their way up to company executive status have proven to be good conversationalists and display a disarming, sincere attitude in spoken English, it obviously does not hold true for the same individuals attempting to communicate to people with a different cultural and language background. Generally, the more senior executives of Japanese companies do not speak English. Note who they are, and be sure to establish eye contact and direct a good degree of your conversation toward them. It will be quickly translated for them, and they will neither feel left out or embarrassed by their lack of English.

Names

The Japanese consider the family as being more important than the individual and write and introduce their surname first. First names are rarely used in Japan. The suffix *san* is the polite form of "Mr.," "Mrs.," or "Ms.," and is used when referring or speaking to supervisors. The suffix *kun* is used for members of the same age group or status, and from superior to inferior. In dealing with you, the foreigner, the Japanese will usually adopt the English "Mr.," with your name. To be safe, it is advisable to address them using "Mr." until you become more familiar with the various nuances of *san* and *kun*. Even Japanese quite younger than you may resent being called *kun*, as it implies a familiarity and a senior-junior bond whose concept and responsibility is outside the scope of most Westerners.

Other Important Points to Consider

Although your Japanese hosts may, in deference to Western custom, ask you to bring your wife along to night-time entertainment, they are probably only being polite. Unless it is a specific cocktail party where all wives are expected to attend, the Japanese would never consider taking along their wives and would feel restrained and uncomfortable in the presence of yours.

The Japanese are inveterate gift givers. Besides the traditional time for giving gifts, at Christmas or year end, there is also a custom of a midsummer gift-giving season called *Chugen*. The most common and popular gift, however, is the *omiyage*, which is a souvenir native to a certain region. Most foreign businessmen receive several *omiyage* from their Japanese hosts. It is a good idea to take along a number of small gifts (souvenirs from your area or scotch) to reciprocate in advance the forthcoming hospitality of your hosts.

The Japanese consider it impolite to open a gift in front of their benefactor. When giving a gift, they will downplay the value of it, saying "it's nothing, just a worthless trinket," or something to that effect. When receiving a gift, they will at first insist that it is not necessary and they will apologize for the inconvenience that you went through in presenting it to them.

Conclusion

Much more could be written about entertainment in Japan. The preceding is intended to give the neophyte a starting point. With experience, the complexities, nuances, and challenges will become clearer.

9

Contract Negotiations

Introduction

*D*ifferences in language, social customs, business practices, and legal regulations between the United States and Japan may greatly increase the complications that sometimes occur in international negotiations. In Japan, the usual practice in business transactions in their domestic market is to keep written agreements to a minimum. But in international trade, particularly for large Japanese firms, the use of appropriately detailed contracts is almost universal. The most common situation in which problems occur in trade transactions with Japan is when two companies, relatively inexperienced in international transactions, begin trade with overly informal or incomplete contractual agreements.

Some of the problems that have arisen are:

☐ Incompleteness or inappropriateness of contract clauses.
☐ Misunderstandings concerning contracts arising from the Japanese system of consensus decision making.
☐ Improper translations and consequent differences in interpretation.
☐ Failure to provide an arbitration clause to permit efficient settlement of claims which may arise because of the dissatisfaction of one party.

Disputes concerning contracts that include an arbitration clause, can be submitted to an arbitration organization, such as the Japan Commercial Arbitration Association (Japan's exclusive organization for this purpose) for settlement.

Contract Disputes

If a Japanese negotiator is asked "What does a contract mean to you?" words which come to his mind are: legal obligations, law suit, indemnities, damage for the company (financially and image). Perhaps this is justified. Recently, for example, when a famous American musician was planning a concert in Japan, the contract document became 1,000 pages. The details included the identification of the model and year of car which was used for his limo, his menu for breakfast, how to cook his eggs, etc. But there were problems and the Japanese promoter was sued and paid $100,000 indemnities.

In Japan, after the signing of the contract, if something is wrong, Japanese try to resolve it by mutual agreement. If disputes arise, the common interests of the two parties, or their relative strengths, are generally the factors that determine the out-

come of any dispute. Japanese businessmen use their intellect, their heart, and their "guts." Business deals negotiated by foreigners are sometimes lost because of a neglect of the heart.

Instead of submitting disputes to a third party, such as a court judge, disputants prefer to settle their differences through discussions with persons who are familiar with their respective situations and problems. The Japanese consider submitting an issue to a court for settlement embarrassing and also find it to be a time-consuming and inconvenient process. Naturally, there are exceptions to this general statement about business agreements. For example, contracts with government ministries are required because of the careful inspection of government expenditures by the Government Accounting Agency. Also, where large sums of money or title to real estate is involved, written agreements are usually required and tend to be written with precision.

But even in fairly detailed contracts there will generally be a clause concerning the settlement of disputes that permits wide latitude for arbitration of disputes. A phrase often found in written contracts might be translated as follows: "All items not found in this contract will be deliberated and decided upon in a spirit of honesty and trust." From a strictly legal viewpoint, a phrase of this type would be acceptable only in cases where the parties to the contract had strong mutual interests and sufficient common ground in their thinking to decide their differences on the basis of "honesty and trust."

With the rapid expansion of Japan's foreign trade during the postwar period, one of the first lessons learned by companies engaged in imports and exports was the importance of precise contracts covering the contingencies that may be experienced. While business agreements in the domestic market still do not commonly require precise written contracts, virtually all foreign trade is conducted with very carefully written contracts that cover a wide range of contingencies and usually include a clause that permits arbitration by appropriate authorites.

Despite the use of contracts in international trade, a number of problems, particularly between Japanese and overseas companies with relatively little experience in foreign trade, continue to occur. Imports and exports handled by larger trading firms and more experienced manufacturing companies very rarely are the subjects of disputes. However, there are still a large number of disputes involving trade between less experienced companies, generally concerning small shipments.

Potential Areas of Contract Disputes

Contract disputes most frequently occur where the Japanese party is unfamiliar in the use of contracts and tends to conduct business affairs through a mixture of the domestic practice of operating without contracts and the more precise method of using contracts covering various contingencies. In the worst cases, contracts have been copied from written sources and may contain inappropriate clauses or clauses that place one of the parties in an unfair position.

Terms of the Contract

A problem that occurs from the beginning of contract negotiations is how detailed the contract should be. Some companies prefer little more than a "gentlemen's agreement," which might consist of only a letter of general terms and conditions of the business transaction. Other firms may prefer contracts that cover every conceivable contingency that might arise. Exactly what contingencies should be covered in a contract depends upon the goods or service being traded and the situation of the parties to the contract. Most contracts for import into Japan should contain statements that address the following:

☐ The transaction will occur, which clearly indicates that the parties to the contract are acting as independent and responsible parties in making the agreement.
☐ The terms and conditions of shipment of the goods. This statement will generally indicate (1) that the bill of lading for the goods will constitute proof of the date of shipment by cable or telex, giving details of contract number, vessel name, sailing date, loading port and invoice amount; and (2) that delay of shipment will be cause for claiming damages, provided a claim is filed in 30 days.

☐ The responsibility of the buyer to obtain an import license, which is required under Japanese law.

☐ The seller's responsibility for payment of duties and other charges that may be incurred in the country of shipment, as well as a statement indicating the treatment of a contingency such as an increase in freight rates after conclusion of the contract.

☐ The amount of insurance to be purchased and the responsibility for arranging for insurance coverage.

☐ The seller's responsibility for the quality and fitness of goods in the buyer's market and the period in which the buyer may file a claim concerning any deficiency in merchandise received.

☐ A disclaimer for conditions beyond the control of both parties (force majeure). That is, where the shipment of goods is detained, destroyed, or the carrying out of the contract is affected by such circumstances as riots, civil commotions, wars, action by government, acts of God, storms, fires, accidents, or other contingencies, the parties to the agreement shall "review the terms and conditions of the contract so as to try best efforts to restore the party or parties to the same relative positions as previously obtained hereunder."

☐ The handling of a breach of contract by one of the parties.

☐ Permission to arbitrate in case any of the terms or conditions of the contract are disputed or contingencies arise not covered by the contract.

☐ The name of the country whose laws will be applied in determining the validity of the contract. A typical statement is the following:

1. This contract shall be governed as to all matters including validity, construction and performance, by and under the laws of Japan.

2. The trade terms under this contract shall be, unless otherwise stipulated herein, governed and interpreted under and by the International Rules for the Interpretation of Trade Terms (INCOTERMS) of the International Chamber of Commerce in force at the date of conclusion of this contract.

Although these items cover the majority of contingencies that might occur, the fact that disputed claims continue to arise as a consequence of misunderstanding or noninclusion of these items is evidence of the need for careful preparation of contracts. Since many disputes occur from misunderstandings that transcend the contract itself, it is advised that an arbitration clause be included to cover those cases that may be unforeseen.

Disclosure of Corporate Information

The question of disclosure of corporate information, either through the content of a contract to the other party or through release of the contract itself to other parties has occasionally been a source of problems. The practice in Japan is:

☐ For the Japanese party to request sufficient corporate information from potential trade partners to evaluate their creditworthiness. Resistance to this minimum requirement makes carrying out trade more difficult and may necessitate provision of guarantees for payment where the Japanese side is the buyer in the agreement.

☐ To follow the requests of the other party to the agreement concerning the secrecy of the contract itself. The two parties to the agreement should reach definite and clear agreement on how the contract will be treated to avoid possible misunderstandings.

Translation and Interpretation

Some written indication is necessary of which version (English or Japanese) of the contract, if there is more than one, will be regarded as the binding one. An arbitration clause generally proves very useful in cases where interpretation of the contract or the question of translation arise as areas of disputes.

Contracts and Decision-Making in Japan

One frequent source of misunderstanding in dealing with Japanese firms is the method of decision making commonly practiced. Although there is a trend to giving increased authority for concluding trade contracts to officers at the *bucho* or division management level, there is still a wide variation among Japanese companies in exactly who has the authority to conclude a trade contract. It is important to note that unlike most Western countries, where the president or his representative may be assigned full responsibility for decision making among a larger group of persons, in Japan final authority for the decision rests with one man, and he is generally unwilling to make a decision until the opinions of the most trusted of his subordinates have been fully considered. For this reason, decision making in Japanese companies usually takes longer than in other nations, and individuals are sometimes not in a position to make a decision on the spot. Therefore, it is important to keep the following in mind in negotiating contracts with Japanese representatives:

☐ As explained earlier, do not expect representatives to make on-the-spot decisions concerning the content of a contract or changes in a proposed contract. Leave time for the representatives to confer with the person having authority to give final approval. Although decisions are slow in the making, they are acted upon quickly.

☐ Remember that because of linguistic differences, "yes" may mean little more than "yes, I understand"; it does not necessarily indicate full agreement with the statements being made or the intention to sign a contract to that effect.

☐ Because of the possibility of misunderstanding arising from purely oral agreements or "gentlemen's agreements," it is generally wise to tactfully insist on a written agreement.

☐ Remember that some smaller companies may be an exception to the rule of group decision making. Just as in other nations, a company with a "one man" president may be accustomed to leaving decisions up to him.

Other Features of Contracts

There are a number of other contingencies and problems which should be considered in preparing trade contracts. Some of these are as follows:

- ☐ Rebates and payments—Contracts will typically contain some specification of the timing and method of payment for merchandise supplied. In Japan, it is not uncommon for manufacturers to pay rebates based on sales performance to distributors, and distributors in turn to retailers. This method of determining these rebates may be included in contracts to prevent possible misunderstanding.
- ☐ Pricing—One pitfall to avoid is specifying retail prices in contracts, since this practice is not permitted except in the case of a limited number of items, such as cosmetics. The buyer and seller normally maintain very close communication on pricing matters and arrive at an understanding.

Conclusion

In conclusion, there are two additional points to keep in mind when negotiating with Japanese businessmen. First, an awareness of how important the development of the personal relationship is to the success of the negotiations. Recognize the cultural differences between Japan's emphasis on harmonious relationships and the American practice of arm's-length bargaining and adversary relationships. The quicker one learns to adapt and use these differences, the quicker he or she will be able to use them to advantage. Secondly, during negotiations it will pay to gauge the degree of commitment expressed by the Japanese counterpart. The Japanese may agree to provisions that are insisted upon, even when they realize they cannot fulfill the commitment. A negotiator aware of this cultural issue should back out upon realization of the position he has placed his counterpart in.

10

Are You Ready?

*T*he material in this chapter allows you to review the important points in the preceding chapters. Since the purpose of the book is to serve as a practical guide for American negotiators working with Japanese negotiators, the five parts in this chapter will help you determine your preparedness.

Part 1—Review Questions
Part 2—Checklist
Part 3—True/False Questions
Part 4—Critical Incidents Test
Part 5—Non-Verbal Exercise

Part 1—Review Questions

These questions are designed to combine and contrast various points made throughout the preceding chapters.

☐ Compare the education and training of a Japanese negotiator versus a U.S. negotiator. What are the implications for *your* negotiations?
☐ What are ten aspects of the Japanese culture that will influence Japanese business negotiators?
☐ Compare and contrast the four basic influence styles of negotiation. What is *your* style?

☐ Explain the basis and the functioning of the Japanese *ringi* system of decision making.

☐ Compare and contrast major differences of the Japanese view with the American view of the goals and priorities of contract negotiations.

☐ List ten American strategies and mannerisms that would be annoying in the negotiation process in Japan.

☐ What are the most important aspects of the initial stages of the Japanese-American negotiation process?

Part 2 — Checklist

Consider negotiation as the process of maximizing both sides' interests. Have you remembered to . . .

Pre-Negotiations

☐ Send as much information before actual negotiation in order to lay the ground work for negotiations.

☐ Use business cards with your name and title in both English and Japanese. This will help the Japanese team determine the position/names and titles of their counterparts.

☐ Use audiovisuals with synchronized recordings in Japanese when appropriate.

☐ Arrange for an "experienced" interpreter; the Japanese respect this and this person can make a significant difference in your ability to negotiate and communicate skillfully.

☐ Select persons on your team with technical skills, negotiating skills, and rapport with other team members.

During Negotiations

☐ Listen carefully. Evaluate their statements before responding.

☐ Communicate clearly. Complicated language and colloquial terms build a barrier between you and the Japanese team.

☐ Use questions to establish their company's needs, to clarify issues, and to consider new alternatives.

☐ Maintain a formal posture, dress, and etiquette throughout negotiations.

☐ Address their entire team and be alert to the fact that the head negotiator may not always be an expert in and/or briefed on all aspects of the proposal.

☐ Regarding the interpreter:
  • Speak slowly for accurate translation
  • Keep him current on all issues
  • Allow time for him to make notes
  • Allow time to clarify points
  • Give rest periods
  • Don't interrupt
  • During long negotiations use two interpreters

☐ Summarize the main points discussed and agreed on during meetings; begin subsequent meetings with a review of these points.

☐ Remember Japanese often require an extended time period to reflect on specific points.

☐ Repeat numbers carefully and write them down to avoid misunderstanding.

☐ Do not use first names. In a business situation in Japan a person is not called by their first name. When you are introduced, clarify what your first and last name is.

☐ Avoid excessive praise of your product or service.

☐ Avoid exhibiting aggressive or confrontative behavior.

☐ Do not engage in arguments; the Japanese will probably refuse to retort, argue, or even discuss a point if he believes he is right. Silence will most likely be their response.

☐ Never put a Japanese negotiator in a position of having to admit being wrong or having failed.

Contract/Post Negotiations

☐ After each meeting spend time debriefing each member of the team.

☐ Be careful when mixing business matters into a social situation; this may be viewed as a pressure tactic.

☐ Be prepared for a lengthy time before the contract will be signed. Do not plan a 2-day trip to Japan. The costs are high and should be properly budgeted.

Part 3 — True/False Questions

Determine whether the following statements are true or false, and know why. The answers follow.

1. Japanese are most comfortable with negotiators who are precise, direct, and to the point from the beginning to the end of the negotiating process.

   T _____   F _____

2. Due to the cultural value of "saving face," Japanese tend not to put anyone on the spot or cause them embarrassment.

   T _____   F _____

3. Japanese will often have their question-and-answer period at the end of a negotiating session.

   T _____   F _____

4. It is important to comment as soon as the Japanese negotiator has finished making a point. This will show interest and understanding on your behalf.

   T _____   F _____

5. Even though Americans are advised not to push for specifics in agreements, the Japanese expect accurate, thorough information supporting a presentation.

   T _____   F _____

6. Details of the contracts should be presented during the negotiations.

   T _____   F _____

7. One of the reasons for Japanese success in the business world is the laissez faire role of government.

   T _____   F _____

8. Japanese have difficulty in understanding someone who argues in order to have an idea accepted or understood.

T _____ F _____

9. Japanese sometimes use the word "problem" or "it will take more time" instead of saying "no."

T _____ F _____

10. The Japanese believe that efforts and achievements speak for themselves and a person does not need to "blow his own horn."

T _____ F _____

11. In Japan, using the index finger and the thumb to make an "O" means O.K. or fine.

T _____ F _____

12. The dedication and loyalty of the Japanese company to its workers are two of the main reasons for Japan's high level of productivity.

T _____ F _____

13. The Western negotiator should inform the Japanese how long he plans to stay in Japan and push for agreement before departure.

T _____ F _____

14. Americans often view business negotiations as a process that can be easily handled by a seasoned and technically proficient negotiator.

T _____ F _____

15. With reference to contract terms, the Japanese may agree to provisions that are insisted upon, even when they realize they may not be able to completely fulfill the commitment.

T _____ F _____

Answers

1. F   2. T   3. T   4. F   5. T   6. F   7. F   8. T
9. T   10. T   11. F   12. T   13. F   14. T   15. T

Part 4 — Critical Incidents

The following questions were designed to test your understanding of appropriate behavior in each of the situations. The
answers follow.

1. Your manager is attempting to relate product features recently acquired through technological advancements.
   These new features would require additional expenditures on the part of the Japanese. In response to your
   proposal, the Japanese say "yes" and become silent. You
   should:
   a. Take this to mean agreement and acceptance of these
      additional costs by the Japanese.
   b. Take this as a negative response to your proposal.
   c. Interpret this as neither positive or negative.

2. After your last presentation on production requirements
   the Japanese become very quiet — many with their hands
   folded or with their hands resting in front of their
   mouths. Your team begins to get edgy. One of your members begins to reiterate one of the points of the proposal.

You, as head negotiator, should:
   a. Help your fellow team member in the explanations.
   b. Ask that the meeting be adjourned in order to be able
      to discuss in private what might be happening.
   c. Signal your fellow member to be quiet and patient.
   d. Ask the head Japanese negotiator what area of your
      negotiation is causing the difficulty in order that you
      might clear up the situation.

3. Your team is expected to report on negotiations in three
   days at corporate headquarters. Eight days of negotiations have lapsed and your team has just begun negotiating the specifics of the contract. The Japanese respond
   by nodding their heads.
   a. You consider their response as agreement to your pro-
      posal.

    b. You sense that the Japanese are becoming uncomfortable.

    c. You should sit back and wait for the Japanese to make counter proposals.

4. Underline unacceptable behavior in the following scenario:

Jim's negotiating team has been invited to dine with the Japanese team at a Japanese restaurant. Jim's team has never eaten Japanese food before. At the restaurant, Jim is a little uncomfortable and very hot, and before sitting down takes his jacket off and loosens his tie. He now feels more at home as he enters a conversation with two members of the Japanese team. As the one member refers to him as Mr. Jim, Jim stops him and tells him to please call him just Jim. The other members begin to settle in around the table. Jim jokes that he has never eaten this low before, and the members of his team chuckle in response. Jim asks the Japanese team leader if there is some way in which it might be possible to come to a compromise over an issue discussed during the day. The conversation is interrupted as the first course of the meal is placed before them. Jim winces as he learns that it is squid and seaweed soup. Jim suddenly realizes that he did not receive a spoon. When the Japanese next to him offers to show him how to use chopsticks, he diplomatically dodges the situation by responding that he is not very coordinated and he had better use silverware.

5. Your marketing manager discovers that a basic component in the Japanese marketing strategy overlooks a major profit area for your company. You should:

    a. Avoid direct reference to the oversight and plan to incorporate it later.

    b. Bring the situation to their attention and carefully explain how the Japanese were in error.

    c. Develop a new proposal that incorporates the oversight and present to the Japanese the following day.

6. Discussions are currently centered on the size of the Japanese monetary investment. Your team has presented your company's investment proposals, and you have established that the project will require more financing by their company in order for the project to be put into production. The Japanese have become very quiet, and you and your colleagues are beginning to feel that the negotiations are breaking down. Your financial expert presses the head negotiator for a response. The Japanese negotiator responds by saying "it is very difficult." Your colleague restates the situation using different wording in order to clarify the situation for the Japanese. The Japanese leader has become very quiet and seems to draw a breath through his teeth and says, "sah." Your colleague is confused and looks at the interpreter for help.

   a. You should try to reiterate the situation by restating your position in simpler wording.
   b. You signal your members to listen.
   c. You ask that the meeting be recessed for the day in order to give yourself more time to figure out what happened.
   d. You move on to another monetary concern.

Answers

1. c 2. c 3. b 4. "before sitting down takes his jacket off and loosens his tie"; "please call him just Jim"; "has never eaten this low before"; "asks the Japanese team leader . . . compromise"; "winces"; "realizes that he did not receive a spoon"; "not very coordinated . . . silverware"; 5. a 6. b

Part 5 — Non-Verbal Expressions

The following expressions may be observed by Americans during negotiations in Japan. These pictures were shown to a group of Japanese businessmen who agreed on the most likely meaning. Under each photo write your interpretation and then check it with the answers.

1. _____

2. _____

3. _____

4. _____

5. _____

Answers

1. Boring
2. Interest
3. Anger
4. Thinking
5. Confidence

11

Meeting the Challenge

Training International Negotiators

*I*n the Foreword of the 1984 Report entitled "What We Don't Know Can Hurt Us" prepared by the American Council on Education by C. Peter McGrath states:

> "We Americans no longer have the luxury of time and distance to justify our lack of concerted attention to the serious and dangerous lag—a shortfall in our international competence."

With the global interdependent economy, it has become imperative to understand our world trade partners. The question that arises now is what can be done to give negotiators a more thorough knowledge of Japan and Japanese negotiators? There are both short and long-term solutions. First, we must recognize that the lack of knowledge U.S. negotiators have for Japan means a loss of business. A remedy for this ignorance is to provide negotiators with experiential training programs involving briefings and cross-cultural communication training. Feedback from Japanese participants as well as videotaped sessions would help negotiators to see themselves in the negotiating process to understand what they might be doing to contribute to ineffective communication.

In terms of long-run solutions for improving cross-cultural negotiations, we must look to the root of the problem in our educational system. If the U.S. is to participate as an effective, respected, and competitive trading partner, our children must be trained in foreign languages. During high school, students should be offered the opportunity to participate in "study-abroad" programs. The language training would continue throughout college, then once again, the student could spend a year in a university overseas (again, preferably in a country that is one of our major trading partners). Ultimately, once the individual is working in a multinational firm, part of his career path would be spent working overseas.

The American Council on Education report found that in 1983 only 15% of American high school students were taking a foreign language. In 1965 the figure was 24%. Unless the trend is reversed, it could be less than 5% by the year 2000.

This long-term plan may be idealistic and requires a financial commitment from today's executives to support and promote international business/language training (i.e., exchange student programs, etc.). If this becomes a priority, we may have many qualified executives skilled in cross-cultural negotiations and this will ensure that international trading partners open their doors more willingly to the United States.

Japan and the Free Market Structure

During the past ten years, the number of complaints from the United States and Europe about Japanese trading practices has increased. Japanese balance of payment surpluses, continual high unemployment in Western countries, and the position of the dollar as the leading currency in the world trade are all factors that are reinforcing this frustration.

Traditionally, Japan is characterized as a country with aggressive export promotions combined with protectionistic measures that exclude some foreign products on the Japanese market. However, the market in Japan is far from closed to foreign products.

The problem is that advanced industrial countries are losing market share in Japan due to declining competitive power. The forms of organization and management practices required for marketing in Japan differ considerably from the European and

American marketing concept. Japanese industry is characteristic in the way that the production function and the marketing function normally are performed by separate organizations. For example, many Japanese companies sell through an independent company that frequently works for a larger group. This system has its origin in feudal times when production was an honorable occupation while selling was not.

The Japanese trading companies are service-oriented. There is also an intimate connection between the trading company, the financing bank, and the industrial group. This interaction has made the trading companies able to establish worldwide networks to handle export/import, financing, joint-ventures, and exchange of technological know-how.

Characteristics of the Japanese Consumer-Market

The mass-consumer market in Japan is larger than the total oil revenues of all OPEC countries put together, and it is ranked as the second largest consumer-market in the free world following the United States. Population concentration in Japan is extremely high. A population half that of the United States is concentrated in an area about the size of California. The high degree of urbanization makes it easy to reach a wide variety of individuals using relatively few types of communication media. The consumers' feeling of closeness and homogeneity makes a rapid spread of information about new products possible.

The Japanese consumer market is continuously changing and changing quickly. In addition to a large and growing population, there are several new population factors that are beginning to significantly influence the mass-consumer market. Upward movement of the age in the population, smaller family units, and more individual families are basic factors that recently have influenced the market-structure.

The trends toward greater individual freedom do create changes in the marketplace. As the group-orientation weakens, individuals begin to make decisions for themselves and base these decisions upon their own welfare, rather than the welfare of the group. The overall result is greater freedom in purchasing behavior as well as greater consumer demand.

The Japanese consumers' high sense of quality has resulted in intense competition among manufacturers in Japan, such that only the best products will be able to maintain any kind of market share. In contrast to Western markets where quality and after-service usually go hand in hand, the Japanese find it cheaper to assure high quality standards and to avoid after-services as much as possible.

The purchasing power of Japanese consumers has increased considerably in the recent years and income is fairly evenly distributed with the middle class accounting for the bulk of income. In spite of opposite predictions, the savings rate has continued to increase and is today approximately 20% compared to 10% for most Western nations.

Advertising

The Japanese consumer is highly receptive to advertising, and believes that it informs consumers about product features and helps them to make intelligent buying decisions. Further, advertising tends to generate prestige for the advertiser and his products.

Research shows that Americans and Japanese react differently to advertising. While Americans react more to the verbal portions of advertisements, the Japanese react more to the nonverbal message portions. In other words, advertising in Japan requires another form of communication; advertising with emphasis or projecting of feelings rather than hard facts. Japan is ideally suited for the use of mass media advertising because the highly concentrated population makes the target groups easy to reach. The prime media used in advertising are television and newspaper, and have a potential to reach virtually 100% of the Japanese population. Almost every household (99%) in Japan has at least one television set. The Japanese mass market consists of consumers who are generally well-informed on current events (the literacy rate in Japan is more than 99%—one of the highest rates in the world).

Distribution System

Distribution is often described as the key factor in the Japanese marketing process. There are two ways to penetrate the Japanese market: (1) use the distribution channels of a trading company or wholesaler; and (2) establish one's own distribution network, which is virtually impossible for foreign businesses. The complexity of the Japanese distribution system has led many foreign companies to forego or even fail in their attempts to penetrate the Japanese markets, although the task of reorganizing and remodeling the distribution system into a more efficient one is a task that both domestic producers and foreign exporters face to an equal degree.

Conclusion

In many ways, the success of a negotiation is determined before the actual meetings even begin. The U.S. negotiator who enters the negotiation unfamiliar with the Japanese system or the background of Japanese negotiators will seldom reach his goals. The challenge is to become a highly competent international negotiator.

_____ **Appendix A** _____

Negotiation Skills

A
Self-Assessment
Exercise *

Please respond to this list of questions in terms of what you believe you do *when interacting with others.* Base your answers on your typical day-to-day activities. Be as frank as you can.

For each statement, please enter on the Score Sheet the number corresponding to your choice of the five possible responses given below:

1. If you have never (or very rarely) observed yourself doing what is described in the statement.
2. If you have observed yourself doing what is described in the statement *occasionally, but infrequently:* that is, less often than most other people who are involved in similar situations.
3. If you have observed yourself doing what is described in the statement about *an average amount:* that is, about as often as most other people who are involved in similar situations.
4. If you have observed yourself doing what is described in the statement *fairly frequently:* that is, somewhat more often than most other people who are involved in similar situations.

*Adapted by Pierre Casse from Interactive Style Questionnaire (Situation Management Systems, Inc.) in *Training for the Cross-Cultural Mind,* SIETAR, Washington, D.C., 1979. Used with permission.

5. If you have observed yourself doing what is described in the statement *very frequently:* that is, considerably more than most other people who are involved in similar situations.

Please answer each question.

1. I focus on the entire situation or problem.
2. I evaluate the facts according to a set of personal values.
3. I am relatively unemotional.
4. I think that the facts speak for themselves in most situations.
5. I enjoy working on new problems.
6. I focus on what is going on between people when interacting.
7. I tend to analyze things very carefully.
8. I am neutral when arguing.
9. I work in bursts of energy with slack periods in between.
10. I am sensitive to other people's needs and feelings.
11. I hurt people's feelings without knowing it.
12. I am good at keeping track of what has been said in a discussion.
13. I put two and two together quickly.
14. I look for common ground and compromise.
15. I use logic to solve problems.
16. I know most of the details when discussing an issue.
17. I follow my inspirations of the moment.
18. I take strong stands on matters of principle.
19. I am good at using a step-by-step approach.
20. I clarify information for others.
21. I get my facts a bit wrong.
22. I try to please people.
23. I am very systematic when making a point.
24. I relate facts to experience.
25. I am good at pinpointing essentials.
26. I enjoy harmony.
27. I weigh the pros and cons.
28. I am patient.
29. I project myself into the future.
30. I let my decisions be influenced by my personal likes and wishes.
31. I look for cause and effect.
32. I focus on what needs attention now.
33. When others become uncertain or discouraged, my enthusiasm carries them along.
34. I am sensitive to praise.
35. I make logical statements.
36. I rely on well tested ways to solve problems.
37. I keep switching from one idea to another.

38. I offer bargains.
39. I have my ideas very well thought out.
40. I am precise in my arguments.
41. I bring others to see the exciting possibilities in a situation.
42. I appeal to emotions and feelings to reach a "fair" deal.
43. I present well articulated arguments for the proposals I favor.
44. I do not trust inspiration.
45. I speak in a way which conveys a sense of excitement to others.
46. I communicate what I am willing to give in return for what I get.
47. I put forward proposals or suggestions which make sense even if they are unpopular.
48. I am pragmatic.
49. I am imaginative and creative in analyzing a situation.
50. I put together very well-reasoned arguments.
51. I actively solicit others' opinions and suggestions.
52. I document my statements.
53. My enthusiasm is contagious.
54. I build upon others' ideas.
55. My proposals command the attention of others.
56. I like to use the inductive method (from facts to theories).
57. I can be emotional at times.
58. I use veiled or open threats to get others to comply.
59. When I disagree with someone, I skillfully point out the flaws in the others' arguments.
60. I am low-key in my reactions.
61. In trying to persuade others. I appeal to their need for sensations and novelty.
62. I make other people feel that they have something of value to contribute.
63. I put forth ideas which are incisive.
64. I face difficulties with realism.
65. I point out the positive potential in discouraging or difficult situations.
66. I show tolerance and understanding of others' feelings.
67. I use arguments relevant to the problem at hand.
68. I am perceived as a down-to-earth person.
69. I go beyond the facts.
70. I give people credit for their ideas and contributions.
71. I like to organize and plan.
72. I am skillful at bringing up pertinent facts.
73. I have a charismatic tone.
74. When disputes arise, I search for the areas of agreement.
75. I am consistent in my reactions.
76. I quickly notice what needs attention.
77. I withdraw when the excitement is over.
78. I appeal for harmony and cooperation.
79. I am cool when negotiating.
80. I work all the way through to reach a conclusion.

Score Sheet

Enter the score you assign each question (1, 2, 3, 4, or 5) in the space provided. *Please note:* The item numbers progress across the page from left to right. When you have all your scores, add them up *vertically* to attain four totals. Insert a "3" in any number space left blank.

1. _____	2. _____	3. _____	4. _____
5. _____	6. _____	7. _____	8. _____
9. _____	10. _____	11. _____	12. _____
13. _____	14. _____	15. _____	16. _____
17. _____	18. _____	19. _____	20. _____
21. _____	22. _____	23. _____	24. _____
25. _____	26. _____	27. _____	28. _____
29. _____	30. _____	31. _____	32. _____
33. _____	34. _____	35. _____	36. _____
37. _____	38. _____	39. _____	40. _____
41. _____	42. _____	43. _____	44. _____
45. _____	46. _____	47. _____	48. _____
49. _____	50. _____	51. _____	52. _____
53. _____	54. _____	55. _____	56. _____
57. _____	58. _____	59. _____	60. _____
61. _____	62. _____	63. _____	64. _____
65. _____	66. _____	67. _____	68. _____
69. _____	70. _____	71. _____	72. _____
73. _____	74. _____	75. _____	76. _____
77. _____	78. _____	79. _____	80. _____
IN: _____	NR: _____	AN: _____	FA: _____

Negotiation Style Profile

Enter now your four scores on the bar chart below. Construct your profile by connecting the four data points.

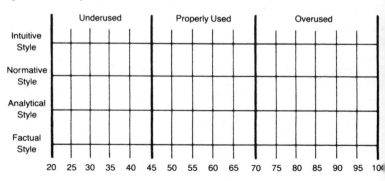

Description of Styles

Factual

Basic Assumption: "The facts speak for themselves."

Behavior: Pointing out facts in neutral way, keeping track of what has been said, reminding people of their statements, knowing most of the details of the discussed issue and sharing them with others, clarifying, relating facts to experience, being low-key in their reactions, looking for proof, documenting their statements.

Key Words: Meaning, define, explain, clarify, facts.

Intuitive

Basic Assumption: "Imagination can solve any problem."

Behavior: Making warm and enthusiastic statements, focusing on the entire situation or problem, pinpointing essentials, making projections into the future, being imaginative and creative in analyzing the situation, keeping switching from one subject to another, going beyond the facts, coming up with new ideas all the time, pushing and withdrawing from time to time, putting two and two together quickly, getting their facts a bit wrong sometimes, being deductive.

Key Words: Principles, essential, tomorrow, creative, idea.

Normative

Basic Assumption: "Negotiating is bargaining."

Behavior: Judging assessing and evaluating the facts according to a set of personal values, approving and disapproving, agreeing and disagreeing, using loaded works, offering bargains, proposing rewards, incentives, appealing to feelings and emotions to reach a "fair" deal, demanding, requiring, threatening, involving power, using status, authority, correlating, looking for compromise, making effective statements, focusing on people, their reactions, judging, attention to communication and group processes.

Key Words: Wrong, right, good, bad, like.

Analytical

Basic Assumption: "Logic leads to the right conclusions."

Behavior: Forming reasons, drawing conclusions and applying them to the case in negotiation, arguing in favor or against one's own or others' position, directing, breaking down, dividing, analyzing each situation for cause and effect, identifying relationships of the parts, putting things into logical order, organizing, weighing the pros and cons thoroughly, making identical statements, using linear reckoning.

Key Words: Because, then, consequently, therefore, in order to.

Guidelines for Negotiating with People Having Different Styles

1. Negotiating with someone having a *factual* style—
   - Be *precise* in presenting your facts.
   - Refer to the *past* (what has already been tried out, what has worked, what has been shown from past experiences . . .).
   - Be *indicative* (go from the facts to the principles.
   - Know your dossier (including the details).
   - Document what you say.
2. Negotiating with someone having an *intuitive* style—
   - Focus on the situation as a whole.
   - Project yourself into the future (look for opportunities).
   - Tap the imagination and creativity of your partner.
   - Be quick in reacting (jump from one idea to another).
   - Build upon the reaction of the other person.
3. Negotiating with someone having an *analytical* style—
   - Use logic when arguing.
   - Look for causes and effects.
   - Analyze the relationships between the various elements of the situation or problem at stake.
   - Be patient.
   - Analyze various options with their respective pros and cons.
4. Negotiating with someone having a *normative* style—
   - Establish a sound relationship right at the outset of the negotiation.
   - Show your interest in what the other person is saying.
   - Identify his or her values and adjust to them accordingly.
   - Be ready to compromise.
   - Appeal to your partner's feelings.

_____Appendix B_____

Information Sources

U.S. Agencies/ Organizations

Advisory Council of Japan-U.S. Economic Relations
Chamber of Commerce of the United States
International Division
1615 H St. NW
Washington, DC 20062
(202) 463-5489

Country Office for Japan
U.S. Department of State
Washington, DC 20520
(202) 632-3152

International Economic Policy (Japan)
International Trade Administration
U.S. Department of Commerce
Washington, DC 20230
(202) 377-4527

Japan-America Society of Washington
1302 18th Street NW
Washington, DC 20036
(202) 223-1772

Japan Economic Institute
1000 Connecticut Avenue NW
Washington, DC 20036
(202) 296-5633

Japan National Tourist Organization
630 Fifth Ave.
New York, NY 10011
(212) 757-5640

Japan Society
333 East 47th Street
New York, NY 10017
(212) 832-1155

Japan Trade Center
1221 Ave. of the Americas
New York, NY 10020
(212) 997-0414

Information Resources in Japan

The American Chamber of Commerce in Japan
701 Tosho Bldg.
2-2-3 Marunouchi
Chiyoda-ku, Tokyo 100,
Japan
(03) 211-5861

The World Trade Center of Japan, Inc.
P.O. Box 57
World Trade Center Bldg.
No. 4-1, 2-chome,
Hamamassu-cho
Minato-ku, Tokyo, Japan

Business Publications on Japan

BI Forecasts of World Markets: Japan
Business International Corp.,
One Dag Hammarskjold
Plaza
New York, NY 10017

Foreign Economic Trends: Japan
International Trade
Administration,
Department of Commerce,
Washington, DC 20230

International Series: Japan
Ernst & Whinney,
153 E. 53rd St.,
New York, NY 10022

Investment in Japan
Peat, Marwick, Mitchell & Co.,
345 Park Ave.,
New York, NY 10022

Japanese Finance and Industry
The Industrial Bank of Japan,
3-3 Marunouchi 1-chome,
Chiyoda-ku, Tokyo, Japan

Tax and Trade Guide: Japan
Arthur Andersen & Co.
69 West Washington St.,
Chicago, IL 60602

Directories on Japan

American Firms in Japan
World Trade Academy Press,
50 E. 42nd St.,
New York, NY 10017

Directory of Japanese Companies in the U.S.A.
Economic Salon, Ltd.,
60 East 42nd St.,
New York, NY 10017

Japan Company Handbook
The Oriental Economist,
4 Hongokucho 1-chome,
Nihonbashi, Tokyo 103, Japan

Japan Economic Yearbook
The Oriental Economist,
4 Hongokucho 1-chome,
Nihonbashi, Tokyo 103, Japan

Standard Trade Index of Japan
Japan Chamber of
Commerce & Industry,
2-2 Marunouchi, 3-chome,
Chiyoda-ku, Tokyo 100, Japan

Bibliography

Books

Abegglen, J. *Management and Worker: The Japanese Solution.* Tokyo: Kodansha University Press, 1973.

Austin, L. *Saints and Samurai: The Political Culture of the American and Japanese Elites.* New Haven: Yale University Press, 1975.

Azumi, K. and C. McMillan, "Worker Sentiment in the Japanese Factory: Its Organizational Determinants," in *Japan: the Paradox of Progress,* ed. by L. Austin. New Haven: Yale University Press, 1976.

Ballon, R. J., ed. *The Japanese Employee.* Tokyo: Tuttle, 1970.

Barlow, W. C. and G. P. Fisen. *Purchasing Negotiations.* Boston, MA: CBI Publishing Company, 1983.

Barnlund, D. C. *Public and Private Self in Japan and the United States.* Tokyo: The Simul Press, 1975.

Bell, R., ed. *The Japan Experience.* New York and Tokyo: Weatherhill, 1973.

Boetner, M. T. and J. E. Gates. *A Dictionary of American Idioms.* Barron's Educational Series, Inc. West Hartford, Connecticut, 1976.

Brislin, R. W. *Cross-Cultural Encounters:* Elmsford, NY: Pergamon Press, 1981.

Brown, B. R. and J. Z. Rubin. *The Social Psychology of Bargaining and Negotiation,* New York, N.Y.: Academic Press Inc., 1975.

Bunge, F. M. *Japan: A Country Study.* Washington, D.C.: The American University, 1982.

Calero, H. H., *Winning the Negotiation.* New York, NY.: (Hawthorne Books, Inc.) Dutton, 1979.

Chang, C. S. "Individualism in the Japanese Management System." *Japanese Management, Cultural and Environmental,* S. M. Lee, Ed. by G. Schwendiman, Praeger, 1982.

Christopher, R. C. *The Japanese Mind: The Goliath Explained.* New York: (Linden Press) Simon & Schuster, 1983.

Clark, R. *The Japanese Company.* New Haven and London: Yale University Press, 1979.

Cohen, H. *You Can Negotiate Anything.* New York: Lyle Stuart, Inc., 1980.

Cole, R. E., *Work, Mobility, & Participation: A Comparative Study of American and Japanese Industry.* Berkeley: University of California Press, 1979.

Condon, J. C. and M. Saito, eds. *Intercultural Encounters With Japan: Communication-Contact and Conflict.* Tokyo: The Simul Press, 1974.

De Mente, B. *How to Do Business in Japan: A Guide for International Businessmen.* Phoenix, 1974.

De Vos, G. "Achievement Orientation, Social Self-Identity, and Japanese Economic Growth," in *Modern Japan: an Interpretive Anthology.* Irwin Scheiner, ed. New York: MacMillan, 1974.

Druckman, D. *Negotiations: Social-Psychological Perspectives.* Sage Publications, Inc., Beverly Hills, CA.

Fayerweather, John and Ashok Kapoor. *Strategy and Negotiation for the International Corporation,* Ballinger Publishing Company, Cambridge, Massachusetts, 1976.

Fisher, G. *International Negotiation—A Cross-Cultural Perspective.* Chicago, Illinois: Intercultural Press Inc., 1982.

Fisher, R. and W. Ury, *Getting to Yes: Negotiating Agreement Without Giving In.* Bruce Patton, ed. Boston: Houghton Mifflin Company, 1981.

Flynn, D. "Japanese Values and Management Processes," *Japanese Management: Cultural and Environmental.* S. M. Lee, G. Schwendiman, eds. Praeger, 1982.

Forgus, Ronald H. and Lawrence E. Melamed. *Perception: A Cognitive-Stage Approach,* second edition. New York: McGraw-Hill Book Company, 1976.

Fourkaer, L. E. and S. Siegel. *Bargaining Behavior.* McGraw-Hill, New York, N.Y., 1963.

Gibney, F. *Miracle by Design: The Real Reasons Behind Japan's Economic Success.* New York: Times Books, 1982.

Gibney, F. *Japan: The Fragile Super Power,* revised edition. Tokyo: Norton Press, 1979.

Hall, E. T. *The Dance of Life: The Other Dimension of Time.* Garden City, New York: Anchor Press/Doubleday, 1983.

Hanan, M., J. Cribbin, and H. Berrian. *Sales Negotiations Strategies.* New York, NY.: AMACOM, 1977.

Harragan, B. L. *Games Mother Never Taught You: Corporate Gamesmanship for Women.* Warner Books. New York, 1977.

Harris, P. R. and R. T. Moran. *Managing Cultural Synergy.* Gulf Publishing Company, Houston, 1982.

Ilich, J. *The Art and Skill of Successful Negotiation.* Englewood Cliffs, N.J.: Prentice-Hall Inc., 1973.

Kapoor, A. *Planning for International Business Negotiation,* Ballinger Publishing Company, Cambridge, MA, 1975.

Kennedy, G., J. Benson and J. McMillan. *Managing Negotiations: A Guide for Managers, Labor Workers, and Everyone Else Who Wants to Win.* Englewood Cliffs, N.J.: Prentice-Hall, Inc., 1982.

Lebra, T. S. *Japanese Patterns of Behavior.* An East-West Center Book. Honolulu: The University Press of Hawaii, 1976.

Lee, S. M. and G. Schwendiman, eds., *Japanese Management: Cultural and Environmental.* New York: Praeger Publishers, 1982.

Leonard, J. T. "Japanese Management; Reasons for Success." *Japanese Management: Cultural and Environmental.* S. M. Lee and G. Schwendiman, eds. Praeger, 1982.

Matsumoto, K. *Organizing for Higher Production: An Analysis of Japanese Systems and Practices.* Tokyo, Japan, 1982.

Moran, R. T., J. Sobin, V. Tyler. "International Business Travel Tools," unpublished manuscript, 1983.

Nakane, C. *Japanese Society,* Berkley: University of California Press, 1970.

Nierenberg, G. I., *Fundamentals of Negotiating.* New York, NY: (Hawthorn Books Inc.) Dutton, 1977.

Norbury, P. and G. Bownas, eds., *Business in Japan: A Guide to Japanese Business Practice and Procedure,* revised edition. Boulder, Colorado: Westview Press, 1980.

Ouchi, W. *Theory Z: How American Business Can Meet the Japanese Challenge.* Reading, Massachusetts: Addison-Wesley Publishing Company, Inc., 1981.

Pascale, R. T. and A. G. Athos. *The Art of Japanese Management: Applications for American Executives.* New York: Simon and Schuster, 1981.

Pruitt, D. G. *Negotiation Behavior.* New York, NY: Academic Press, 1981.

Seward, J. *More About the Japanese.* Lotus Press, Japan, 1971.

Sours, M. H. "The Influence of Japanese Culture on the Japanese Management System." *Japanese Management: Cultural and Environmental.* S. M. Lee and G. Schwendiman, eds., 1982.

Stewart, E. C. *American Cultural Patterns: A Cross-Cultural Perspective.* Society for Intercultural Education, Training and Research, Intercultural Press, 1971.

Strauss, A. *Negotiations: Varieties, Contexts, Processes, and Social Order.* San Francisco: Jossey-Bass, Inc., 1978.

Tyler, V. L. and J. S. Taylor. *Reading Between the Lines—Language Indicators Project.* Eyring Research Institute. Provo, Utah, 1978.

Vogel, E. F. *Japan As No. 1: Lessons for America.* Cambridge and London: Harper and Row, 1980.

Wilkinson, E. *Misunderstanding: Europe vs. Japan.* Tokyo, Japan: Chuokoron-sha, Inc., English Language Edition, 1981.

Articles

Alexander, P. "Fighting It Out," *Time Magazine,* August 1, 1983.

Angelmar, R. and Stern, L. W. "Development of a Content Analytical System for Analysis of Bargaining Communication in Marketing," *Journal of Marketing Research,* February 1978, pp. 93–102.

Block, Z. "Joint Venturing in Japan," *The Conference Board Record.* April 1972, pp. 32–36.

Bonoma, T. V. and Felder, L. C. "Nonverbal Communication in Marketing: Toward a Communicational Analysis," *Journal of Marketing Research,* 1977, pp. 169–180.

Dahlby, T. "Anatomy of Japan: the Businessman," *Far Eastern Economic Review,* April 24, 1981, pp. 76–80.

Drucker, P. F. "What We Can Learn from Japanese Management," *Harvard Business Review.* March–April 1971, pp. 110–122.

Fields, G. "How to Scale the Cultural Fence," *Advertising Age,* December 13, 1982, Sec. 2, pp. M-11 and M-12.

Foltz, K. and N. Ukai, "Headhunting in Japan," *Newsweek,* (November 7, 1983), 110.

Graham, J. L. "A Hidden Cause of America's Trade Deficit with Japan," *Columbia Journal of World Business,* Fall 1981, pp. 5–15.

Graham, J. L. "Brazilian, Japanese and American Business Negotiations," *Journal of International Business Studies,* Spring/Summer 1983, pp. 47–59.

Graham, J. L., R. A. Herberger, Jr. "Negotiators Abroad—Don't Shoot from the Hip," *Harvard Business Review,* July–August 1983, pp. 160–168.

Greenwald, J. "The Negotiation Waltz," *Time,* August 1, 1983, pp. 41–42.

Harriman, W. A. "Observations on Negotiating: Informal Views of W. Averell Harriman," *Journal of International Affairs,* Spring 1975, pp. 1–6.

Hawkins, S. "How to Understand Your Partner's Cultural Baggage," *International Management,* August 1983, pp. 28–31.

Hopper, K. "Creating Japan's New Industrial Management: The Americans as Teachers." *Human Resource Management,* Summer 1982, pp. 13–34.

Jastram, R. W. "The Nakodo Negotiator," *California Management Review,* Winter 1974, Vol. 17, No. 2, pp. 88–90.

Johnson, R. T. and Ouchi, W. G. "Made in America (Under Japanese Management)," *Harvard Business Review,* September/October 1974, pp. 61–69.

Johnston, R. W. "Negotiation Strategies: Different Strokes for Different Folks," *Personnel,* March–April 1982, pp. 36–44.

Klein, H. "Firms Seek Aid in Deciphering Japan's Culture," *Wall Street Journal.*

Kohan, J. "Talking Past Each Other," *Time Magazine,* August 1, 1983.

Lohr, S. "The Business Card: A Japanese Ritual," *The New York Times,* September 14, 1981, Sec. 4, 1.

Main, J. "How to Be a Better Negotiator," *Fortune,* September 19, 1983, pp. 141–146.

Marengo, F. "Learning From the Japanese: What or How?" *Management International Review,* Vol. 19, No. 4, 1979, pp. 39–47.

Masao, Kunihiro, "Indigenous Barriers to Communication," *The Japan Interpreter,* Winter 1973, pp. 96–108.

Mathews, H. L., Wilson, D. T. and Monoky, J. F. "Bargaining Behavior in the Buyer-Seller Dyad," *Journal of Marketing Research,* February, 1972, pp. 103–105.

Matsumoto, H. "Our Experience With an American Company," *Conference Board Record,* April, 1972, pp. 35–37.

Morrow, L. "All the Hazards and Threats of Success," *Time Magazine,* August 1, 1983.

Nierenberg, G. I. "What You Should Know About Negotiating," *Management World,* October, 1982.

Nishiyama, K., Ph.D. *Communication in International Business.* Honolulu, the University of Hawaii, 1967.

Ohmae, K. "Japan's Entrepreneurs Battle the Goliaths," *The Wall Street Journal,* December 20, 1982, p. 17.

Pascale, R. T. "Communication and Decision Making Across Cultures: Japanese and American Comparisons," *Administrative Science Quarterly,* Vol. 23, March, 1978, pp. 91–109.

Pennington, A. L. "Customer-Salesman Bargaining Behavior in Retail Transactions," *Journal of Marketing Research,* August, 1968, pp. 255–262.

Reischauer, E. D. "The Japanese Way," *Across the Board,* December, 1977, pp. 34–42.

Saadat-Nejad, A. "Factors Which Influence the Transfer of Management Practices Between the United States and Japan." Ph.D. Dissertation, United States International University, 1981.

Sayle, M. "The Yellow Perit and the Red Haired Devils." *Harpers,*
  November 1982.
Shimaguchi, M. and W. Lazer. "Japanese Distribution Channels:
  Invisible Barriers to Market Entry." *MSU Business Topics,* Win-
  ter 1979, pp. 49–62.
Tsurumi, Y. "Myths That Mislead U.S. Managers in Japan," *Har-
  vard Business Review,* July–August, 1971, pp. 118–128.
Van Zandt, H. F. "How to Negotiate in Japan," *Harvard Business
  Review,* November–December 1970, pp. 45–46.
Ways, M. "The Virtues, Dangers, and Limits of Negotiation," *For-
  tune,* January 15, 1979, pp. 86–90.
Wells, L. T. "Negotiating with Third World Governments," *Har-
  vard Business Review,* January–February, 1977, pp. 72–80.
Whitney, G. G. "Before You Negotiate: Get Your Act Together,"
  Personnel, July–August 1982, pp. 13–26.

Newsletters

"A Case Study of Foreign Investment in Japan," *JETRO* Market-
  ing Series 3, New York: Japan External Trade Organization.
A Hundred Things About Japanese. Japanese Culture Institute,
  1975.
"Doing Business in Japan," *JETRO* Marketing Series 8, New
  York: Japan External Trade Organization.
Japan: A Businessman's Guide prepared by the Financial Times,
  London. American Heritage Press, New York.
"Japan as an Export-Market." Jetro Marketing Series #1.
Sales Promotion in the Japanese Market." Jetro Marketing Se-
  ries #7.
"Side by Side Negotiations," *Personnel Journal,* August 1982, p.
  556.
"The Dance of Negotiations," *Time,* December 7, 1981, pg. 111.
"The Fine Art of Negotiation," *Security Management,* February
  1983, p. 70.
"The Japanese Consumer." Jetro Marketing Series #6.
"The Japanese Market in Figures." Jetro Marketing Series #10.
"Thoughts on Negotiation," *Harvard Business Review,* July–Au-
  gust 1983, p. 168.
"Understanding the Japanese—If That's Possible," *JETRO Busi-
  ness Information Series.* Printed in Japan.

Recommended Reading

I recommend that the following fine books on Japan be read next and in the order listed:

Graham, J. L. and Yoshihiro S. *Business Negotiations John Wayne Style: And Other Problems for Americans Bargaining in Japan* and *Smart Bargaining: Doing Business with the Japanese,* Cambridge, MA: Ballinger Publishing Company, 1984.

Lee, S. M. and G. Schwendiman, eds. *Japanese Management: Cultural and Environmental Considerations,* New York: Praeger Publishers, 1982.

Condon, J. C. *Interact: Japanese and Americans.* Chicago: Intercultural Press, Inc., 1983.

Hall, E. T. *The Dance of Life: The Other Dimension of Time,* Garden City, New York: Anchor Press/Doubleday, 1983.

Tung, R. L. *Business Negotiations with the Japanese,* Lexington, MA: Lexington Books, D.C. Heath and Company, 1984.

Index

Getting Your Yen's Worth

Here is an incisive, no-nonsense, fast-paced guid to successfully negotiating with some of the be businessmen in the world. While much has bee written about doing business with "Japan, Inc.", n where will you find a more practical source of accu rate, relevant, and understandable information f going "head to head" with America's most com petitive trading partner.

This compact reference clearly describes the optimum appearance, behavio and negotiating tactics for American executives to use and, just as important, explains how Japanese executives perceive such efforts. The book orients th reader with some historical and cultural background but primarily focuses on ne gotiating styles/techniques that should and should not be used, including execu tive's negotiating posture, proper social interactions, and key words/concepts criti cal to understanding the Japanese negotiating style.

Only from an author who knows the country (Moran lived in Japan for fiv years), the language (he is fluent in Japanese), and the psychology of cultural in teraction could come such straightforward and valuable insights into successfull negotiating with the most industrially aggressive nation on earth, "Japan, Inc."

Robert T. Moran, Ph.D., has been a trainer and consultant to more than 100 internationa companies including ARCO Exploration, J. I. Case, Chase Manhattan Bank, Control Date Honeywell, FMC, Exxon Chemicals Asia Pacific, Aramco, and Volvo. Co-author of *Managin Cultural Differences*, 2nd edition, Dr. Moran is currently professor of international studies an director of the program in cross-cultural communication at the American Graduate School International Management in Glendale, Arizona.

Cover design by David Pric

ISBN 0-87201-410-